"A deeply human story of mo[...] [neces]sary to navigate a world not [...] act of love." *Hannah Lavery*

Praise for Catherine Simpson's p[revious books:]

"A superb memoir ... heart-rending ... interwoven with welcome portraits [that] are laugh-out-loud funny." *Sunday Times*

"Riveting and bleakly funny ... compassionate and beadily observed." *Richard Benson, The Observer*

"Witty at times, yet precisely moving ... gripping and heart-wrenching. It sticks with me still." *Mail on Sunday*

"A poignant memoir ... a precise and skilled writer ... a considerable achievement." *Cathy Rentzenbrink, Times*

"If you loved Tara Westover's *Educated*, get yourself a copy as soon as humanly possible ... [a] beautifully understated ... elegiac portrait of farming life in modern Britain." *Vogue*

"A joyful, angry, beautiful air-punch of a book ... I felt as though each word was written on my own body." *Kirstin Innes*

"A vivid framing of the mystery, confusion and even terror tangled up with our young bodies in the '70s." *Mary Anne Hobbs*

"*One Body* is fresh, insightful and moving, and it's a book that every man should read." *Graeme Macrae Burnet*

"Funny, bold, wry and, at times, enraging in the best possible way ... imbued with spirit and a real passion for life." *Mary Paulson-Ellis*

"By turns poignant and searingly honest ... a wise and witty reflection on all that it means to have a body." *Claire Askew*

"Brave and elegiac." *Editor's Choice, Bookseller*

"(Simpson) vividly and thoughtfully unpicks the circumstances in which she and her sisters were raised." *Times Literary Supplement*

"Deeply engaging, courageous and human." *Graeme Macrae Burnet*

"Moving but never mawkish, and ultimately hopeful, a sympathetic portrait of ... autism." *Sunday Mirror*

"Vivid, perceptive and acute." *James Robertson*

"Remarkable ... just wonderful." *Janice Galloway*

Also by Catherine Simpson

Non-fiction
When I Had A Little Sister
One Body

Fiction
Truestory

Hold Fast

*Motherhood,
my autistic daughter
and me*

Catherine Simpson

Saraband

Published by Saraband
3 Clairmont Gardens
Glasgow, G3 7LW
www.saraband.net

Copyright © 2025 Catherine Simpson

All rights reserved. No part of this publication may be reproduced, stored in a retrieval system, or transmitted, in any form or by any means, electronic, mechanical, photocopying, recording, or otherwise, without first obtaining the written permission of the copyright owner.

ISBN: 9781916812512

1 2 3 4 5 6 7 8 9 10

Printed and bound in Great Britain by Clays Ltd, Elcograf S.p.A.

The views and opinions expressed in this book represent those of the author and reflect her personal experience. They do not constitute any professional advice and do not necessarily reflect the official policy or position of any other organisation. The author and publisher accept no responsibility or liability for any of the information contained herein.

There are no known safety hazards associated with this product. Saraband's EU authorised representative is UPI 2M PLUS d.o.o., Meduliceva 20, 10000 Zagreb, Croatia. e-mail neno@upi2mbooks.hr

For Cello, Nina and Lara

In memory of my dear friend
Jane Watson,
who understood and encouraged me to write
about these events as they were happening.

Prologue

This book is about motherhood and, in particular, about the first eighteen years of raising an autistic child – my daughter, Nina.

In Greek mythology, there is a robber called Procrustes who kills his guests by forcing them to lie on an iron bed and cutting their legs short if they are too tall for the bed or stretching them if they are too short. Either way, they die. This procrustean system of demanding utter conformity is reminiscent of how autistic people are often treated in our inflexible neurotypical world where 'difference' is apparently to be avoided lest you be feared, shunned, mocked or judged.

The world tried to cut us off at the knees by demanding that Nina change as a child and I change as a mother. Nina, however, remained resolutely and triumphantly Nina-shaped whether the world (or I) liked it or not. I, though, did change: I learned a lot, and all of it from mothering both my autistic child and my other daughter, Lara.

Motherhood is often portrayed as a world of contentment and joy; it remains difficult to be honest, open and unsentimental about the actuality. For me, the myths of motherhood crashed headfirst into the reality.

Nina, Lara, my husband Cello and I survived this journey and eventually thrived, and this is the story of how we did it.

One

'Mother of two.'

In my thirties, those three words ran through me like the word 'Blackpool' runs through rock.

I was also a journalist, a thrifter, an upcycler, a tap dancer, a bibliophile, a secret would-be novelist, an over-confident arm wrestler, a jewellery-wearer, and a perennial dieter. I had been called a 'bluestocking' and asked if I was 'one of them feminists', but all that was by-the-by in my thirties because by then, my identity was summed up in those three words: 'mother of two'.

To different people at different times, I have been Catherine, Cathy, Caffy, Cath, Miss Simpson, Ms Simpson, or occasionally Cello's wife or Mrs Mega – a married name I never adopted – but for a generation of kids and parents at the school gates, I was Nina's Mum or Lara's Mum.

I learned years later from a Palestinian taxi driver called Abu Shaddi that in Arab cultures, they adopt honorific nicknames upon the birth of a child: 'Abu Shaddi' meaning 'Father of Shaddi'. Our system may not be as formal, but it is as sure.

When neighbours, a generation older, asked if my journalist husband, Marcello, known as Cello, could witness some legal documents I said, no, *I* would do it. Next to 'Occupation', in what felt like an act of defiance, I wrote 'Full-Time Mother'. I sensed surprise from them both, tinged – I like to think – with approval from the wife.

When people asked if I was embarrassed to be labelled a full-time mother – which they did – I refused to acknowledge embarrassment as a possibility, although I realised that not many women wanted to identify themselves first and foremost as such in 1995.

'Housewife', however, was a word I abhorred and seemed like a term from the worst of times, but I was proud to be a mother.

Women had always been mothers, hadn't they?

Being a daughter never defined me like being a mother did. Being a daughter wasn't central to who I was – although being a farmer's daughter came close.

I never wondered if I was a good daughter. I never considered what a good daughter might be. My dad, a dairy farmer, was a peaceful man and asked only that my sisters and I did not thump each other or yank each other's hair out, which necessitated us doing so in silence.

He was agitated by raised voices and avoided anything that could 'end in tears'. He recoiled from violence on the television, and in the seventies thought the Palestinian boys should just stop throwing stones. He remembered with a fond chuckle that as a lad, he'd doffed his cap to the parson and was a royalist who was proud that his father had been invited to Buckingham Palace. He hated confrontation, much to my mother's frustration, who snapped 'Not throw stones! What else are they supposed to do?! The other side have *guns*!' Mum rolled her eyes at the very idea of doffing your cap to anyone and stated baldly that she 'wouldn't go to t' garden gate to see t' Queen Mother'.

Mum was a full-on, fly-off-the-handle confrontationalist; a woman for whom the exclamation mark was invented.

Dad himself fought using silence and head shaking and a few muttered 'Eee, I don't knows', while my mother fought with hard words and, when they failed, a silence that crept from under her bedroom door and settled heavy over the house.

One

My parents had been married a year before they had my sister Elizabeth, four years when I was born, and seven years when Tricia arrived. Despite their great differences, I saw Mum and Dad as a unit because they were *married*.

And to be married apparently meant you stuck together for life, whether you liked it or not.

Letters arrived addressed to Mr & Mrs JS Simpson – my mother, it seemed, had no name, merely a title: 'Mrs'. She rolled her eyes at the custom of making married woman disappear and insisted that the farm business and bank accounts should be in the name of JS & MA Simpson.

One day, I heard her furious with Dad because she had heard him refer to her as 'the missus' to a visiting sales rep. 'I am nobody's missus!' My mother believed that unless you were very careful, being a married woman in the seventies lacked dignity.

My mother was living a life that was too small for her. Before she married in 1959, she had sung professionally, but she suffered from debilitating stage fright so had turned down the chance to get an equity card. When she left school, her father offered to set her up as a dress maker, but she turned him down, telling him he needed her at home on the farm.

She was a farmer's daughter who became a farmer's wife. She never really fitted the mould and often seemed frustrated and angry at life.

I remember sitting in the back seat of the Austin Princess with my sisters, Dad driving and Mum beside him. 'As a girl, you must always have something to fall back on,' my mother said over her shoulder. Above the passenger seat, I could see her fox fur collar, the one with the little pinched glassy-eyed fox face attached to it, so this must have been a New Year's Eve outing to Aunty Margaret's.

'What have you got to fall back on, Mummy?' I asked innocently, and I saw her silhouette as she looked at Dad and did a little laugh at being caught out.

One Sunday evening, Dad came into the farmhouse from the milking parlour carrying a stainless-steel jug of frothing milk straight from the cows. My sisters and I were sitting around the kitchen table, our felt pens spread out, listening to the radiogram, diligently listing the top twenty in specially hand-decorated notebooks. When Radio 2 DJ Tom Browne said '...and at number four in this week's chart, it's *Swing Your Daddy* by Jim Gilstrap', Dad danced along in his wellies and big work-jacket encrusted in muck and straw, swaying the jug from side to side and grinning, which might not have been exactly what Jim Gilstrap had in mind.

On the other hand, when Ed 'Stewpot' Stewart played *I saw Mommy Kissing Santa Claus* on *Junior Choice* one Saturday morning as Mum stood at the oven bringing the milk to the boil, she rolled her eyes at the sheer banality of life, the universe and everything in it.

It took me years to realise that Mommy in the song was not really kissing Santa Claus at all, but Daddy in a Santa suit. I found it easier to believe in Father Christmas.

My dad taught me words like 'yer little tykes' and 'jiggered' while my mother taught me words like 'puerile', 'fractious', 'enunciate', 'insolent' and 'aggravate'. They both called us 'pie-cans'. I knew what they meant when they said 'stop being a pie-can', but only now, aged 59, do I think to seek out a definition.

Pie-can: northern English for a clumsy, stupid, foolish, person; a dope.

Mum also called us 'sluts' in the old-fashioned sense of the word – 'a woman of slovenly and untidy habits'. She could be a traditionalist at times, my mother.

One

Being a daughter to my dad was a different experience to being a daughter to my mother. My mother did not make motherhood look like much fun.

Motherhood would be different for me, I decided. I would ensure *that* by sheer strength of will. For a start, I vowed never to tell my children to 'get out from under my feet' or to 'stop mithering', or worse, to 'stop prating', and none of my children would ever, *ever* be labelled a 'mither-cart' or told to 'dry up'.

'I want three!' I used to say airily, being from a family of three siblings and unable to fathom anything else.

I believed I was made for motherhood, and I couldn't wait to prove it.

And that was my first mistake: believing that I had to prove anything to anyone.

Two

I had known I wanted children ever since my sisters and I pushed a rusty doll's pram around the cobbled farmyard which, judging from the black and white photographs, could have been anytime from the Dark Ages to the Victorian era. It was a tableau straight from a horror film; the pram piled high with armless and legless dolls, dolls with or without eyes, dolls with wobbly heads and chewed heels, dolls shorn 'to see if the hair would grow back', dolls half-naked, dolls completely naked, dolls with clothes felt-penned on, dolls with underwear made of masking tape.

Many people are afraid of dolls – there's a name for it: pediophobia – but I was desensitised early. I loved those dolls, as stiff, cold and unbending as they were, because at least they were sort-of humanoid. Fluffy teddies or plastic dinosaurs did not cut it. Our dolls were cherished and some even had dresses. They had names too: June, July, Big Mary, Little Mary, Sylvia. Sylvia had an expensive, fancy name because she had silver curls and an expensive, fancy blue velvet frock. Sadly, Sylvia was not mine – she belonged to my little sister, Tricia.

I never had a common or garden Barbie, nor a Sindy, but instead the lesser spotted Tressy. She had wild staring eyes and a belly button that, when pressed, let you yank a length of long hair from the top of her head, and with another press would wind it back in again.

For my ninth birthday, Mum said I could choose whichever Tressy I wanted. I chose blonde Tressy, but Mum said no, I could choose brunette Tressy, because brunette Tressy was 'better'. I called brunette Tressy Sandra after the brunette Sandra in *The Liver Birds* and made her one-roomed houses

Two

out of cardboard boxes with furniture from matchboxes and toilet roll holders. Tressy Sandra once moved into a block of flats, like the cool Liver Bird Sandra. The block of flats was actually the middle shelf of the dilapidated toy cupboard in the 'playroom', and the playroom was actually a pre-central heating, damp and sagging lean-to filled with layers of festering, abandoned toys and with the odd woodlouse in the corners.

It was necessary to have a good imagination to play with our dolls.

Caring for our dolls and creating their houses was a poverty-stricken business – the *Blue Peter* world of craft projects and art supplies was from a better-equipped, shinier, more child-friendly world than ours. That world was run by the smiling 'here's-one-I-made-earlier' Valerie Singleton, not by my harassed 'get-out-from-under-my-feet' mother.

No sticky-backed plastic ever darkened the door of our farmhouse. And there were no squeezy bottles either (which were necessary for many *Blue Peter* projects) because my mother cleaned our kitchen with industrial bleach from the dairy and didn't believe in wasting her life washing up, investing in one of the earliest dish washers in the area instead.

As I watched the beguiling world of *Blue Peter* (which seemed colourful even on our black and white telly), I often wondered what even *was* a stamped, self-addressed postcard, and where would a seven-year-old find such a thing? Not in my world, that was for sure. The only postcards I encountered were from Grandma and Grandad on one of their many foreign holidays to Portugal or the Rhineland (on which they would have drawn a cross on their hotel bedroom window, and noted, gaily: 'We are here!').

Children with *Blue Peter* badges were, it seemed, living in a parallel universe, perhaps with those other 'lucky' children who were awarded *Jim'll Fix It* badges; the sort of children whose dreams appeared to have come true. None of those children ever crossed my path.

At almost sixty years old, I still own my dolls – Mary, Diane and Karen are still here, sitting in the attic.

When I am gone, my daughters will have to dispose of all my dolls, plus their dolls too. And dolls are not the only things I have kept. I also have my children's old Halloween costumes – tiny punk rocker vests I decorated with chains and safety pins. I have piles of their drawings and paintings from nursery through to A Level, much of it framed and on display in the house. A friend once studied this framed art and remarked, 'You really celebrate your children, don't you?' I have boxes of farm animals and soft toys, stacks of *Pokémon* and *Yu-Gi-Oh!* cards, that have moved house with me. I thought I had done well getting rid of the old *Harry Potter* tapes, until I found them stacked on top of a wardrobe. The longer you keep this stuff, the harder it gets to throw out.

I have seventy-six family photograph albums lined up in the attic, telling the story of my children's lives.

When I left university, as a mature student aged twenty-eight, I was listed in the yearbook as 'The One Most Likely to Become an Italian Mama and Have Seven Children', which, I thought, didn't sound too bad.

I got married at thirty with the intention of having a baby as soon as possible, and I became pregnant with Nina straight away.

Once I got over the morning sickness, I dived headfirst into preparations: I amassed pregnancy books with their lists, charts and diagrams, and eagerly attended health visitor

Two

appointments to be weighed and measured and prodded and assessed. It was 1994 – pre-Google days – so I gathered leaflets at the doctor's surgery and sought advice by word of mouth.

Despite hating milk, I had a milky drink every day (for calcium for the baby's bones and my teeth) and cut out soft unpasteurised cheeses (for fear of Listeriosis and miscarriage), and of course alcohol was abandoned (to prevent all kinds of horrors on a list as long as your arm). I was reassured that my bread contained folic acid (to help prevent spina bifida). I got a craving for apples, and I stocked up on ginger tea, mint tea and raspberry leaf tea, because… Well, I can't remember exactly why, and I'm not sure I knew even then.

It was a full-time job growing this baby.

I browsed Mothercare stores for expandable clothing and looked forward to being sixteen weeks pregnant and having a reason to wear a shapeless sack. Those were the days when pregnancy bumps were 'concealed' in vast, baggy, gathered, pleated smocks with great white Peter Pan collars 'to draw the eye', Princess Diana style. Princess Diana's pregnancies were a decade before mine but her influence on pregnancy chic remained strong.

In 1991, three years before I was pregnant, Demi Moore had appeared seven months pregnant, naked, sexy – reminiscent of a ripe mango – on the cover of *Vanity Fair* with the headline 'MORE DEMI MOORE'. But Demi Moore did not live in a Lancashire village – nor, as I did by then, the Edinburgh suburb of Morningside. Even for a Hollywood actress, Demi exposing her naked bump had been outré, and the world had been open-mouthed, with some newsstands censoring it. It took a few more decades before non-Hollywood women started to wear Lycra to enhance their bumps, and in my world, by the time Nina was born in 1995, the baggy A-line smock still held sway.

Hold Fast

I compiled lists of names for girls and names for boys: Caitlin, Nina, Rosa, Ruby, Joe, Patrick, Jack, James, consulting my *Name Your Baby* book to check out meanings and asking adult Ninas and Joes what those names had been like at school.

'The name's been good,' said one adult Nina, 'except for boys making police siren noises in the playground: neenah neenah neenaaaaaah!'

I wanted the name to be 'Italian enough' to sit right with an Italian surname, without going strictly traditional because in Cello's ancestral village, it seemed most of the boys were called Marino and the girls Giovanna.

Choosing a name is not to be taken lightly.

Cello told me about a man he knew from his village in Southern Italy who went to register the name of his umpteenth daughter. When he got back, his wife asked him what he had chosen, and he answered 'Caterina', to which she replied, 'We've already got one of those.'

Someone else told me the story of her father being dispatched to the registry office with strict instructions about the intended name, only for him to return having named her after his former girlfriend.

I wasn't inviting suggestions from anyone else or handing over this responsibility. I still shuddered at the memory of my great Aunty Peggy insisting her nephew be named after his grandfather, Walter, to become a boy forever known as 'Wee Walter'. I wasn't trusting this job to anyone – like everything else in this motherhood game, I was excited, enthusiastic and determined to get it right.

I decorated the spare room in our Edinburgh tenement to create a nursery, with all the hopes and dreams that entailed. I painted the eleven-foot-high walls bright yellow and stencilled

Two

tumbling blue wisteria all round. This being the mid-nineties, *everything* in the nursery was stencilled, stippled, sponged, distressed or appliqued within an inch of its life, including my husband's childhood wardrobe, which went from 1960s Formica brown to bright yellow, stencilled and lined with yellow tartan paper.

I handmade soft toys, painted little chairs, and collected books, mobiles, toys and baby bricks from the charity shops, and arranged them as though it was a show home.

Everything, it seemed, was an opportunity for the baby to learn – wall hangings contained detachable letters of the alphabet: 'A is for Apple, B is for Banana…' Another wall-hanging had a teddy declaring, 'I can count' with pockets for One Orange, Two Apples, Three Bananas…

Toys were preferably made of wood. There was, it seemed, something moral about a toy made of wood – wooden toys screamed 'My child does not waste time merely *playing* with lumps of plastic because my child is always *learning*.'

There was even a shop called the Early Learning Centre packed to the gunwales with wooden toys – educational toys – which was a place of pilgrimage for middle-class parents, and it was difficult to fight your way to the shelves of wooden bricks and puzzles and trainsets on a Saturday afternoon.

The books waiting in my baby's nursery were classics – *Grimms Fairytales, The Best of Hans Christian Anderson, A Treasury of Winnie the Pooh*, all the building blocks of a perfect nursery, a perfect childhood.

The room I was decking out as a nursery used to be our lodger's bedroom, and during that era had been a rather spartan environment of rows of polished shoes for the lawyer's office, spiked golf shoes for the golf course and ski boots for the slopes. The lodger, Wayne, was an old friend of Cello's from university and had been there before me, and it had felt strange elbowing my way into this bachelor flat and making it at least partly my own.

I had owned my own home since I was nineteen – for ten years, by then – and I was used to making all the décor decisions myself. I had embarked on sharing living space with Cello with some trepidation. But no sooner had Wayne been ousted (sorry, Wayne) and all our wedding gifts been carefully arranged – a full set of white china, every type of crystal cut glass you could imagine, matching cutlery, matching bedding, matching towels – than it began to be overlaid with baby stuff.

Now, a pile of tiny white vests-in-waiting sat on the painted, stencilled, stippled bookcase, and was topped with a yellow suit, hand knitted by my mother to bring the baby home in.

The stage was set – the curtain (Laura Ashley yellow fuchsia, trimmed with sky blue to go with my sky-high expectations) was ready to be raised, the costumes were prepared, the props were arranged, the backdrop was painted, and there was a huge sense of anticipation. All we needed was the star of the show. This was going to be the greatest production the world had ever seen.

I gave up my job – of course I did. It was motherhood all the way for me from now on. I was going into this new experience wholeheartedly and was not someone who thought babies wouldn't change anything.

I knew babies would change everything and I couldn't wait.

I look back now and I realise that I had no idea how all-encompassing 'changing everything' could possibly be.

At the time, I had no doubt that full-time motherhood was what I wanted. No maternity leave for me, no hedging my bets, no giving myself the chance to 'reconsider my options'

Two

in a year's time. No, the only thing to be done was to recruit my Fundraising Manager replacement, return the keys to the company car, and hand in my resignation letter. Bye bye, career. It wasn't that nice knowing you. I'm over and out and on to better things, things I will be *good* at.

Had I been oversold the idea of motherhood? If so, I think I had oversold it to myself. Where did I pick up this idealised view of motherhood? Not from the home in which I was raised, where motherhood had looked like an exhausting chore.

It was true, though, that within my extended family, even if it didn't look much fun, motherhood *did* come with status. All those childless great aunts and great uncles, although loved, were never quite in the centre of things. It appeared that to be fully respected, a man must have a farm and a woman must have a family. It was only when we were all adults, many years later, that we realised that lovely Uncle Gerald (my dad's brother), who was physically disabled and had no farm, no wife and no children, had never even been asked to be a godparent to any of his nephews and nieces.

On the other hand, my grandmother – a mother of eight, a grandmother of forty-odd and a godmother to who knew how many – had appeared to be the centre of the world.

'Pregnant' had been a word too explicit for my grandad – he had been dead twenty years by this time anyway – but my mother, who *was* a good daughter, said, in the acceptable parlance, 'Catherine is expecting.'

But expecting what?

More than a baby, that was for sure. I was expecting the 'Ideal Family' (in quote marks and spoken with emphasis – *that* kind of ideal family), although I can't envisage exactly what I imagined the 'Ideal Family' to be.

Was it the Ladybird book *Janet and John* mythology of a family – mum at home, dad at work, two parents and two children (probably a boy and a girl – although I wanted girls), children who always smiled and busily co-operated with each other? Was it the advertisers' fantasy of mother in a pinny serving delicious roasts to an oohing and aahing family? Was it a sitcom family? Surely not – at least not the Royle Family, nor indeed the Royal Family, come to that.

I once served on a jury where a mother and stepfather were accused of attempting to murder their two children and each other, on what should have been a family film night after a day of playing in the paddling pool and cooking brownies. The crime scene photographs of the family home showed a decorative crossword on the wall, incorporating all their names, including the names of their two dogs, Kadie and Kodie. The crossword was headed up 'Our Family'. The parents were found guilty. So not that type of family, either.

I *knew* that motherhood would give me meaning and purpose. I wanted someone I could love, someone I could make happy, someone I could give the best of the good things I'd had, and all the good things I hadn't. This was an achievable utopia, surely? Motherhood would be a place where I could be at home and feel right in my own skin. I could harness all my energy and create perfection. Golden slumbers would indeed kiss my baby's eyes and 'smiles await them when they rise', and I would never tire of singing them that lullaby.

Was my life empty before motherhood? No, but I imagined that life after motherhood would be everything I already had (marriage, home, travel, family, friends) *and so much more*. I had grown up in books and wanted my happily ever after. I wanted to feel needed and to be good at something.

Two

Life, without the prospect of having children, felt long and empty. Work had never given me satisfaction – except for the social life and wage packet that came with it. Whether as a civil servant, a local journalist or a charity fundraiser, or before that a shop worker or a barmaid, I had not found meaning in it.

I had not yet had the courage to write creatively, which *would* eventually give me meaningful work, but in 1995, being a writer was a pipedream and an embarrassing pipedream at that; a pipedream that I had confessed to only a few close friends over the years, and then as the years passed, had hoped they'd forgotten.

Instead, I had fallen into jobs rather than choosing them. When I ended up at HM Customs and Excise, my mother's religious friend took a deep breath, looked sad, and said, 'Never mind. Matthew was a tax collector.'

After a few years tax collecting, I had returned to full-time education and trained as a journalist but found the atmosphere of the newsroom to be macho and off-putting, so went to work fundraising for a charity instead – a charity that cared for autistic children, as it turned out.

I considered myself a feminist and saw no conflict with being a feminist and a mother. I didn't think I had to choose between being a mother or being true to myself because being a mother for me was the truest thing of all.

Motherhood was my choice, not my inevitable destiny.

I never considered that in having a child, I was burning my old life down. I never considered what I was giving up. I never thought about the loss of freedom – I mean, what had freedom ever done for me? It had mostly felt meaningless, empty and lonely. I never considered that I would lose my sense of self, because I had never heard of such a concept, and even if I had, I wouldn't have known for sure that I should have one.

All I knew was that I would love this child like I had never loved anyone before.

I was naive about a lot of things, but I wasn't wrong about everything.

I never articulated exactly what I thought motherhood would be like – to myself or to anyone else – but it was something to do with warmth, love, fun, closeness, sharing. A warm home with a warm kitchen, with warm baking and a warm baby, with a lot of smiling – images that I think I may have absorbed from children's books. Beatrix Potter maybe, or *Wind in the Willows*, *Little Women* or Enid Blyton.

In fact, my favourite children's book was *Pippi Longstocking*, a girl who had no parents to speak of, lived alone with a revolver, a bag of gold, a horse and a pet monkey, and was answerable to no one. But by 1995, I had temporarily forgotten Pippi, and I thought that with dedication and love, nothing could go wrong in the creation of my perfect family – and even if it did, any problems could be solved with ingenuity and effort, and oh, was I prepared to put in the effort. I could make this work – I could make this family *perfect and perfectly happy*.

How could a human baby live up to these expectations?

As a child, I had wanted the world to be uncomplicated and straightforward, like a picture book. I had wanted it to be in block colours, solid green grass, solid blue sky, two white fluffy clouds like sheep, a postman in a red van, a farmer with a pitchfork and one brown cow: a life simplified, a fantasy, an illusion, a delusion.

It was into this fictitious uncomplicated landscape that I would deliver a real-life baby.

Two

However, my subconscious must have been sounding a warning: I kept dreaming about putting my swaddled baby down on the floor of the bus for a moment only for it to end up rolling about under the seats, like a rugby ball just out of my reach, my fingertips scrabbling to grab it, as the driver drove faster and faster, lurching round corners, losing control of the bus.

Three

The family I grew up in provided safety – because there is safety in knowing your place.

My place was second of three daughters born into a family of farmers who had worked the same land for three generations, and nearby land before that. When I asked exactly how long our family had been farmers, my mother said 'forever' in a tone that did not imply forever was necessarily a good thing.

My mother was the eldest of eight siblings; my father, the eldest of five. We had cousins coming out of our ears, spread across this village, the next village, and all the way to Canada. I remember the headmaster of the local primary school saying about my cousin, Elaine, 'Everybody at this school calls Elaine's dad "Uncle Dennis". *I'm* going to start calling Elaine's dad Uncle Dennis!'

Our roots were deep and wide. I was a tiny part of a big whole. There were Bens and Marys and Davids and Margarets weaving – or perhaps knitting and purling, crocheting and tatting – the generations together. On Grandma Mary's living room wall was a black and white photograph of three generations of Bens, and now we have a fourth. On Dad's side, there were two generations of Marjories, but when my grandmother Marjorie died giving birth to Aunty Marjorie, who then died herself at twenty-one, there were no more Marjories.

But it was a strange safety: I belonged, but I belonged awkwardly. I was a serious watcher rather than an enthusiastic partaker. In my immediate family, I knew that my place was to keep quiet and not to ask for things, not to take up space or demand attention.

It is possible to feel lonely in a crowd.

Three

Outdoors was my dad's space, indoors was my mother's space. *My* space was inside books – any books I could find, to be read anywhere I could hide, inside or out, up a tree, on a roof, behind the bedroom curtains on the windowsill, or buried under the eiderdown.

Books were portals to other worlds via lustre jugs, faraway trees, wardrobes or clocks chiming thirteen, and I would gratefully step through those portals into magical realms, to a soundscape of either my mother sewing furiously on the old, pale-blue Singer, crashing pots and pans in the kitchen, or singing Schubert at the grand piano in a rich Kathleen Ferrier contralto voice, or to the sounds of my father clanking buckets, revving the tractor or to the lowing of cows and the muted clatter of their hooves on the lane as they were brought up for milking – a sound I can still hear to this day – followed by the hum of Dad switching on the thrumming milking machine.

As regular as clockwork, morning and evening, the cows came up from the fields, the milking machine struck up, and Dad went on. He seemed indefatigably reliable, reliably indefatigable.

I was born in the *annus mirabilis* of 1963, the year National Service was abandoned, and the year sexual intercourse began, according to Larkin. I doubt there was much of a sexual revolution in our corner of Lancashire, despite national events that year including the introduction of the Pill, the Profumo scandal, the release of *Dr No* and the Beatles' hits coming thick and fast. In the week I was born, Brian Poole and the Tremeloes were number one with *Do You Love Me?*, having pushed the Beatles' *She Loves You* out of the number one slot.

There was a lot of singing about love, at least.

If 1963 was a watershed for sex, it wasn't for parenting, and certainly not in our community where things continued in the traditional manner – children should be seen and not heard, and were largely incidental to day-to-day life. Farming families had three or four children, hoping for a boy or two – something my parents never achieved.

Life was about the farm; everything revolved around the twice-daily milkings, and around the weather, the seasons, and the animals.

We had two or three short caravan holidays when I was a child, but we never went abroad – except to Scotland, which my sisters and I considered 'foreign'. When I was seven years old, Elizabeth and I were sent to Grandma and Grandad's farm at the other end of the village for a few days so Mum and Dad could go on a National Farmers Union trip to Germany and Switzerland.

In my school diary, I wrote, 'Mum has a new trouser suit, necklace and earrings. I have a new toothbrush,' and I wondered why the class teacher laughed.

By contrast, when Nina and Lara were small and loved the children's television programme *Balamory* we took them on holiday to Tobermory, the setting for the show.

'There's Josie Jump's house!' I said as we unloaded our cases from the car. I was determined excitement levels should be high, but the kids took it all in their stride, like it was an everyday thing to go on holiday to a CBeebies set. The hotel in Tobermory was the most expensive hotel we had ever stayed at, a fact we noted ruefully as the receptionist slammed down our door key onto the reception desk – 'Your key!' – and disappeared without another word.

'Maybe we'll see PC Plum,' I suggested, still trying to be super-enthusiastic, refusing to let go of the idea that this

Three

holiday was a dream come true. As we entered our 'family room', Nina gazed upon the four-poster draped in regal purple. 'It's the Queen's bed,' she declared, impressed at last.

The Tobermory/Balamory memory demonstrates that not only were we indulgent parents, but that in the years between 1963 when I was born and the 1990s when I gave birth, there had been an about-turn in parenting. My mother had seven siblings, my father had four, but by the time I was in the market for a baby, I would have considered having more than three to be an unusually large family. By 1995, this parenting revolution had put this smaller number of children front and centre, children were everything – they were their parent's world.

I remember an aunt (who had had six babies of her own) coming to visit when Nina was a toddler. She had looked around at the number of toys Nina had in a great trunk in the living room, at her mini blackboard set up beside it, at the shelves and shelves of children's books, at the piles of Disney videos on the television, at the tiny child's desk by the kitchen table, and had marvelled, 'We just let 'em grow up. Now, it's so complicated.'

Why did I feel the need to inundate my children with toys? Was I trying to create a sense of abundance I had not experienced as a child? Or was I trying to make my children like me? Or maybe I thought being surrounded by brightly coloured toys would create a sense of safety, love and security.

I suppose it seemed complicated to my aunt, a generation older than me, because since she had had her children, somebody somewhere had decided that childrearing must be child-centred. Life had become something for children to enjoy and adults to facilitate. Somewhere along the line, parents had turned into child entertainers.

The simpler times were when I was a daughter, not when I was a mother.

Hold Fast

My parents had had no notion of being children's entertainers. My mother gave us a new drawing book and a set of felt pens at the beginning of the summer holidays, and we were thrilled. Beyond that, we played outside making dens, dressing up and riding imaginary horses, and when the weather was bad, we watched television. We watched so much television that if all else failed, we'd watch the testcard. To us as kids, Brian Cant and Valerie Singleton were like family.

Four

I started my formal training to be a mother at antenatal classes. Childcare had been a subject taught at high school – but only for girls not doing O Levels in academic subjects. I, on the other hand, didn't even know where the childcare classroom was. Practical subjects were looked down on as things you did if you couldn't do 'proper' lessons like physics and French. Apparently, trigonometry, logarithms and periodic tables were going to be more useful to the 'clever' ones in our adult lives than knowing how to look after another human being.

Despite having numerous younger cousins, I had hardly held a baby before I gave birth, let alone walked around with one, bathed one or been responsible for one.

I had a memory of a friend of my aunt's placing her naked newborn baby in the middle of the farmhouse kitchen table, a big clip with dried blood attached to its belly button, as she and my aunt examined it closely, puzzling over the state of this feeble thing. My aunt wrinkled her nose at it. I could barely see over the table's edge but decided they were considering whether this coiling and uncoiling creature was worth keeping or not. It certainly looked like a sad specimen to me. A half-cooked, raw, mewling thing, not like the calves and piglets born on the farm that could stand and feed and exist straight away.

My mother shared no information about childbirth except referring to women who insisted on giving birth without anaesthesia as 'being a martyr to it'. I think she had drawn a veil over the entire thing. She even said she could not remember on which day we had been born. I discovered years later that I was a Wednesday's Child and therefore 'full of woe', so maybe my mother was just being diplomatic, especially as my big sister was a Friday's Child – 'loving and giving' – and my little sister was a Tuesday's Child, 'full of grace.' Although, no, that can't have been it because my mother didn't do diplomacy. She must just have forgotten.

Both of my children would be born on a Sunday and as 'the child that is born on the Sabbath Day is bonnie and blythe, good and gay,' I was delighted that at least I'd got that right.

My father's mother had died in childbirth, but that had been such a traumatising event in the family that no details were disclosed, and the subject not discussed. The only mention I remember was my mother remarking 'she was overweight' as if that explained everything. It was years later, when my older sister was training to be a midwife, that I discovered my grandmother had died of pre-eclampsia.

But that kind of tragedy was from another era, surely, and held no fear for me.

What did they tell me at antenatal classes after I had dutifully huffed and puffed up the hill, seven months pregnant, with great anticipation?

They told me how to bath baby. How to test the temperature of the water with my elbow – why my elbow and not my hand? I don't know, they didn't tell me that. How to cradle baby's head in the crook of my arm and trickle water over baby's scalp. How to use different pieces of cotton wool to clean baby's face and bottom. How to always clean baby's face first.

They did not tell me why 'baby' didn't need a definite article now I had one inside me.

They told me there were things I 'must' do.

I must start as I meant to go on.

I must get baby outside in the pram every day.

Four

I must sleep when baby slept.
It seemed motherhood was built of musts.

They told me I must breastfeed, that 'breast was best', because:
- it was convenient
- and easy
- and cheap
- and natural
- and full of antibodies
- and magic.

It was best…just because.

And other dogma, like pain in labour should be controlled by correct breathing. If you ended up in pain, you were breathing wrong – and this in the Simpson Memorial Hospital named after Sir James Young Simpson who pioneered anaesthesia in childbirth, a man who risked his life testing chloroform on himself and his friends during dinner parties down the road in Edinburgh's New Town. A man who woke up after knocking himself unconscious overnight in his dining room and realised that the 'delightful results' of chloroform could control pain in childbirth, despite the church's view that pain was all part of the necessary tribulation of giving birth.

If only Sir James had known about the breathing, he could have saved himself and his pals a lot of bother.

I remember the matronly midwife at the antenatal classes, snug in a blue dress with neat white trim and flat shoes. I don't remember her face or her name, just her *presence*. Her solid, no-nonsense, authoritarian presence.

There was a whiff of basic training in that room; a drilling of raw recruits, a knocking into shape – all into the same shape: the shape of worried, compliant young mothers.

We were the spring birth intake, with due dates at Easter, like a field full of in-calf heifers.

'Spring is a sensible time to give birth!' the midwife declared. 'I cannot understand anyone giving birth in *Feb-ru-ary!*' We all grew a couple of centimetres in our chairs, proud to have inadvertently done something right that pleased this bossy woman.

We introduced ourselves. One woman said she was called Paul-line.

The midwife frowned. 'So, your name is Pauline?'

No, explained the woman, her father was in the merchant navy and had written to say that the new baby must be christened Pauline. But by the time he arrived home six months later, they realised he had got the name Pauline from a book and thought it was pronounced 'Paul-line'. So, from that moment, Paul-line she became and remained.

'Alright…Pauline,' said the midwife.

There was to be none of that Paul-line nonsense in *her* classroom.

The focus of the classes was on getting the baby out and the immediate aftermath, but there was no discussion of the months or years after that.

What else didn't they tell me at antenatal class?

They didn't tell me I was handing my whole life over to fate, to the capricious gods of good and bad luck because I was about to give birth to someone that I would love more than myself, more than I could imagine, but someone I couldn't protect from the vicissitudes of life, from the cruelty of other children, from unkind adults and from the outside world.

They didn't tell me that like any parent, I was forever hitching my peace of mind to that of another.

They didn't tell me I was now a hostage to fortune.

They didn't tell me that.

Cath, an old college friend with a penchant for tarot cards and horoscopes, sent me a prediction: 'Your child will be reckless, impulsive and headstrong…a loving, enthusiastic extrovert who will make your Scorpio hair stand on end. You have been warned!'

I blundered on in a cloud of optimism and hope, not able to articulate any worries or doubts even to myself. One day as I was walking through John Lewis, I felt a searing pain rip down my belly, as though I had been unzipped. I grabbed my bump, but it seemed intact. Just then, I saw an acquaintance waving at me over the stacks of expensive bedding. I waved and smiled back, trying to catch my breath from the sudden hot agony in my abdomen while hiding that anything was wrong. I semi-slumped over a linen display and tried to make conversation without clutching my belly.

I learned later from a book that I had experienced abdominal separation, or *diastasis recti*, when the two long parallel stomach muscles separate due to the pressure of the growing baby. My friend in the shop was pregnant too, due at the same time as me – her third – and she was making it look easy, hardly noticing it, too busy with her first two. I said nothing to her then nor ever told anyone afterwards – no need to make a fuss, no need to make heavy weather of it, just get on with it like it seemed everyone else was.

Like many, maybe most, new mothers, I left the labour ward physically and mentally traumatised. It wasn't so much the pain: I have a high pain threshold – although even so the pain had been strong enough to induce an out-of-body experience

– but more than that, it was the *violence* and the dehumanising lack of control. I was full of suppressed anger, and with incipient post-natal depression.

They didn't tell me about that either.

I had taken the writing of my birth plan very seriously. I had stated that I would like to try a water birth, for pain relief, but if that 'didn't work' then I wanted a pain-killing epidural. All that talk of breathing my way through labour had not impressed me much.

When I arrived in the labour suite, the midwife looked at the great empty birthing pool, put her hands on her hips and said, 'So, you want me to fill *that*?' It suddenly seemed like a huge imposition – it was enormous. How much warm water would *that* take? We gazed at it together, and I agreed, no, maybe not.

I was struck by no matter how extraordinary this day was for me, it was nothing but another routine day for the medical staff.

'Maybe we could go straight for the epidural?' I suggested, but Saturday night, Sunday morning is not epidural territory. Anaesthetists appeared to be thin on the ground in the small hours, so I didn't get that either. Birth plans, it seemed, were ways to distract and falsely reassure the mother beforehand, only to be cast aside on entering the labour ward, along with the ineffective Bach's Rescue Remedy and the Enya cassettes.

I had no voice in the labour ward; nobody listened to me. No matter how many times I asked for an epidural, I kept getting fobbed off. Gas and air did not work – maybe because I was too distressed by then to take deep breaths. My strongest memory is of being told they were going to do an episiotomy – and seeing them wielding what looked like my mother's kitchen scissors.

Four

There was no privacy. Nurses were coming in and out to share in-jokes and chats with each other and creating quite a hubbub. The lights were harsh and dazzling. I felt helpless, vulnerable and very unsafe.

I couldn't leave the hospital for a week afterwards because I struggled to get Nina to feed. When my Italian mother-in-law, Rosa, turned up with a sandwich of home-roasted red peppers wrapped in a bread bag and shoved in her handbag, I could have wept at the humanity of it.

The maternity ward, like the labour ward, was loud and inhospitable. We joked that the metal tea trolleys, piled with jangling teaspoons, had square wheels, and it appeared to be someone's job to push one of these trolleys up and down the ward, world-without-end, forever and ever, like an eternal, everlasting one-man brass band.

The experience of the maternity ward felt like being kicked when I was down, and their insistence that I remain there for a full week was like being taken hostage.

By the time the birth was over, the antenatal preparation and anticipation seemed to belong to a different planet, to time immemorial, and all that appeared to be important to anyone now was that the baby had been safely delivered and that she had ten fingers and ten toes.

If you mumbled about any birth trauma, you were brushed off with 'Oh, that's normal for a first birth…It could have been a lot worse'. So many women have given birth that it is considered ordinary, commonplace, an everyday occurrence, and yet it is not ordinary, it is extraordinary.

Several of my friends were pregnant by then and I didn't want to be the bearer of bad news or be accused of being over-dramatic by being honest with them. Or, for the friends who were yet to get pregnant, I didn't want to be accused of having put them off. So, I wore the accepted public face of pleased and proud new mother, and I joined the conspiracy of silence around birth, implying that all that really mattered was having a healthy baby.

This *omertà* – this code of silence around the reality of motherhood – is broken only occasionally and can be quite shocking when it is. Years before becoming a mother myself, an old friend confided late one night: 'I love my kids, but they have ruined my life.' She took another slug of wine and shook her head and I laughed, unsure what else to do, because I knew she was telling the truth.

So maybe it wasn't a conspiracy of silence, more a wilful deafness on my part.

Likewise, Rosa, my mother-in-law, who adores her grandchildren but spends her life worrying endlessly about all that could go wrong for them, told me emphatically as I nursed my baby, 'If I live again, I no getta married,' then with a slice of the hand, 'and no children!'

But by then it was too late.

After giving birth, whenever I heard that someone was pregnant, my initial thought was 'poor thing', although I always managed to hide this reaction with the expected 'Fantastic!' Upon hearing that a friend was pregnant when Nina and Lara were little, I wrote in my diary: 'Thank God it's not me.'

A long time after giving birth, I learned that there was such a thing as a birth reflection service offered by the NHS where you could meet up with a midwife and discuss any negative thoughts or 'unhelpful feelings' you had about your birth experience. I'm doubtful that this service existed in 1995, but since

Four

finding out about it, I've often thought, is twenty years after the birth too late to ask for the birth reflection service? Is twenty-five? How about thirty?

As I had arrived at the hospital to give birth, I had waddled past a white stretch limo waiting outside the maternity unit full of pink 'It's a girl!' balloons. I was amazed. Who would think of organising such a thing in the midst of the chaos of childbirth?

This was a time before we documented our lives on social media – maybe nowadays, everyone leaves the labour ward in a limo and puts it on TikTok?

Not usually a demanding person, when it came time for me to leave the hospital with Nina, I insisted that she could not be transported home in my old Ford Fiesta – a relic from my civil service days that had not been cleaned in ten years and had rust edging every panel and moss growing round the window. My company car had gone back when I had given up my job, so my father-in-law's Nissan Cherry was requisitioned for the day. There were no balloons, and a stretch limo it was not, but at least it was clean.

One good thing about the ability nowadays to announce a baby's birth on social media and share a few photographs is that it hopefully cuts down on the succession of visitors who used to appear in the nineties. What a terrible idea that was. My advice to would-be visitors is to leave it a while…maybe until the child starts school.

One afternoon a few days after I had escaped from the hospital, friends of Cello's arrived, and I plastered on my best smile. When Nina was crying, I felt anxious and fraught in front of these guests, who had raised a family of their own and surely knew how *wrong* I was getting it – and when she was quiet, I felt resentful that I couldn't just lean my head back and shut my eyes. Cello asked if they would like a coffee – the correct answer from the visitors would have been 'Yes, we'll make it', but Cello is made of different stuff to me. He ran through a menu of coffee varieties on offer – would they like an espresso, perhaps? A filter? Maybe a cappuccino? – until I nearly burst out, 'Just make the fucking coffee so I can go back to bed!'

A savvier friend didn't visit us but sent flowers already arranged in a vase – 'because I know you won't have time to arrange them yourself'.

Among the many gifts of tiny dresses and oh-so-cute doll-like shoes, soft toys, homemade blankets crocheted with love, and nursery accessories a-plenty, a gift arrived from Hugh Collins, a journalistic contact of Cello's. Hugh had been convicted of a gangland murder in the seventies and become known as 'Scotland's most dangerous prisoner' but had turned his life around with art therapy in the Special Unit at Barlinnie Prison. Cello had helped with the campaign to get him released from jail after sixteen years inside. Hugh sent us one of his artworks, a huge, framed charcoal drawing of a faceless swaddled baby. It arrived on its own in a black cab, delivered from Edinburgh, overwhelming and brooding.

Five

As a first-time mother, I felt obliged to look sharp! and do everything that was expected of me, DO IT PERFECTLY and do it *now*. I'm not sure who I thought was watching and judging me, but I felt their hot breath right over my shoulder.

I fell at one of the first fences of motherhood – the Becher's Brook of baby care, the 'notorious and controversial obstacle' of breastfeeding. I crashed out in a welter of shock and cries of pain (both mine and the baby's). Even worse than that, I sometimes resorted to feeding Nina by putting her in a carry cot with a bottle of warm milk propped on a cushion for her to suck on.

'I don't think you're supposed to do that,' commented a visitor, tentatively, as she peered into the cot. 'She might choke'.

But we were learning that sometimes we just had to do what we had to do – like carrying her facing outwards dangling over one arm like the Queen's handbag. This looked a little too insouciant, but at least it stopped her crying because (we surmised) she liked the pressure on her stomach.

Likewise, two health visitors arrived one day when we were still in bed, and I had to root under the blanket to retrieve a sleeping Nina. They exchanged glances and one asked, wide-eyed, 'She's sleeping in bed with you? Like that?' To which I replied, 'Yes. If she sleeps at all,' and they exchanged further looks.

Nina, we would learn, was not destined to be a blind follower of rules, and to keep up with her, we were fated to follow suit.

I took Nina to a mother and baby group at a local church hall because I believed it was something that mothers were *supposed* to do. It felt like a *Stand By Your Beds!* moment. A stand to attention moment. An inspection of raw recruits. A rite of passage for new mothers. It was good for us, we were told, good to mix, good to get out of the house, good for our mental health.

Or maybe we were expected to turn up to prove to the world that we could get ourselves and our baby out of the house at all – or that we were in fact both still alive. I wasn't really sure and nor was I sure who was monitoring this – the health visitors? Other mothers? Society at large? but I knew I should, I *really should* go along. Nina's future welfare may – somehow – depend upon it.

I set off to the local church hall apprehensive but cautiously optimistic. I knew no one. Nina cried. Instead of joining the other mothers beside the hot water urn and the instant coffee and plate of Digestives, I sat cross-legged on the floor holding Nina alongside the other kicking babies. Nina still cried. She didn't like it here – was it the noise? The smell? Could she sense I was tense, self-conscious and uncomfortable? Maybe she knew we'd both be better off outside, or in a café watching the world go by, or at home on our own, or indeed anywhere else but here. Her crying upped a gear until she cried so much, she vomited and not just a little bit, not a posset, but a fountain.

The smiles dropped from the other mothers' faces, and they abandoned the tea urn to stride over and snatch their babies away as though I had just clanged a bell and shouted, 'Unclean! Unclean!' I remained on the rug trying to console my crying baby and another mother handed me a shaggy-headed floor mop, and I thought, *what the fuck am I supposed to do with that?* I cleared up the sick with a stack of tissues taken from my beautiful blue changing bag – a gift from a friend – a bag that had been packed for weeks before the birth, ready for all the exciting outings we were going to go on.

Five

I felt like an outcast; cast out. Nobody spoke to me, I spoke to nobody. I kept my head down and tried not to cry until I could get out of there, head home, and never go back.

Cello had a month off work when Nina was born. A surreal month during which time night became day, day became night, and sometimes we would give up trying to sleep at all and sit in bed in the lonely, disconnected small hours clutching undrunk cooling cups of tea, shell-shocked.

It would take us all day to get ready to go out, only for us to realise by the time we were ready to leave the flat, it had gone dark.

'Where will you go at this time on a Sunday night?' asked my sister and I confidently replied that Waterstones, the book shop on Princes Street, would still be open. It wasn't. We were all dressed up with nowhere to go, so we went nowhere.

There is tremendous pressure to 'get the baby into a routine', which is gaslighting of the first order. A baby is a baby is a baby and feeds when it needs. Years later, a young couple came to stay with us, bringing their newborn with them. They were devotees of Gina Ford and were *waking a baby to feed it* to a strict schedule, which was an act of madness in my opinion.

As surreal as our experience had been, it did not seem harder than this particular young couple with their intense desire to 'get it right' and their determination to get the baby into a routine, come what may, an aim that produced stress so intense it resounded through us all like the highest note on a tuning fork.

A month after Nina was born, Cello rejoined the real world (at least during the day) by returning to his previous life as a journalist – an office life, a newsroom life, a life with colleagues, lunch hours, gossip and shared jokes, with expenses for entertaining journalistic contacts, with trips away, with bylines and picture bylines, with awards and prestige – and I stayed at home, having willingly turned my back on my own office life.

And very soon, motherhood began to feel like it was me and Nina against the world.

It is often implied that being a stay-at-home mother is so boring it turns you into a dullard. According to memoirist Annie Ernaux, 'mothering and the life of the mind seem incompatible'.

This doesn't give quite the right impression to me.

I found mothering to be physically and emotionally exhausting, that was true, but also hugely mentally challenging, with a series of insurmountable problems to solve every day. It was a much harder job than any I had ever received a salary for. There were so many things to get wrong as I tried to work it out day by day, feeling my way along blindfolded, with so much at stake.

I found it impossible and demanding, impossibly demanding, demandingly impossible. I felt taut and stretched to the limit rather than bored, saggy and lacking stimulation.

The dizzying image of those plate spinners, entertainers who regularly appeared on television in the seventies – men in tuxedoes and bow ties who kept umpteen plates spinning at once on top of thin canes while grinning broadly and trying to look like they were enjoying themselves – was never far from my mind. But unstimulating? Never.

There is a saying: 'Every time a baby is born, a mother is born too.' There is a word for this process of becoming a mother – the physical, psychological and emotional changes you go through after giving birth: 'matrescence.' A word I never

Five

encountered until years after I had lived through it twice. A word that my spell check in 2024 still does not recognise and tells me does not exist.

Nina started smiling when she was a tiny baby. 'It's just wind,' said the experts, insisting that babies could not smile so young. But it wasn't wind. As she lay on a cushion, and I tickled her lips with the teat of her baby bottle, she smiled and smiled and smiled as I laughed, and Cello took photographs. When I look back at the photos, I see a baby most definitely smiling – smiling with her eyes as well as her mouth – and I am angry all over again at those who would kill the joy and deny a mother a smile.

Nina smiled and enjoyed cuddles and splashing in the bath and being rocked in her seat, but she could also get inconsolably distressed for long periods, crying and crying, and most difficult of all, she hardly seemed to sleep. There were times during the night when I wasn't sure if the cries I heard – cries that echoed round my head and round the flat – were real or imaginary. I thought I was going mad, but learned later that phantom crying is not uncommon in anxious new mothers.

I had to make many tricky decisions each day, calculating how to minimise her distress. I constantly scanned the horizon for potential problems, making snap judgements. Where was it 'safe' to take her? Where would she be content? Where would I be most likely to keep her happy? It was hard to know what might trigger her distress.

I was constantly on duty, hypervigilant, and getting increasingly exhausted and depleted by the day.

Regardless of that, though, I remained keen to 'get it right' because such is the pressure on new mothers. I was metaphorically still that raw recruit shining my boots and standing by my bed waiting for inspection for months, possibly years, after Nina was born.

I bought a thing called a moule which in 1995 was the in piece of equipment for new mothers – middle-class ones, at least – and which enabled me to squash cooked fruit and veg through a sieve and then freeze the mush in ice cube trays for handy meals. Looking back now at the chaos of pots and pans and peelings and ice cube trays all over my kitchen table, the word 'handy' no longer seems the most appropriate. But back then I was guided by a book, which became a sort of bible, written by a beautiful woman who was photographed on the back cover in her pristine white kitchen. This woman was an influencer long before social media came into being, and years before the word 'influencer' appeared in the Oxford English dictionary.

She didn't just advocate mouleing bog-standard carrot and apple either: there were 'recipes' for sweet potato and squash, lychee, mangos and paw paw, cantaloupe and papaya. Some of these foodstuffs I had never tasted myself – and judging by the terrible smell of the paw paw, I probably never would. No packets, jars or artificial food for my baby, oh no, even if this shopping, peeling, chopping, cooking, mouleing and freezing rigmarole was one of many pressures contributing to a frenzied feeling of *will I ever be good enough?*

One day, I was sitting at a friend's table. Her two older children were eating scrambled egg for tea and my friend was cuddling her baby who was the same age as Nina. After the older children had left the table, my friend took the now-cold left-over scrambled egg from the other children's plates with her fingers and popped it into the baby's mouth, and he happily ate it. As I got up to leave, I pictured the lychee/paw-paw/baby rice extravaganza that was waiting for Nina at home, and

Five

I asked her what her baby would be having for his tea. My friend shrugged: 'Well, he's had that egg.' And I marvelled at how much easier it appeared to look after a third child than a first – without realising that there was no law prohibiting me from taking an easy way out too.

Having married into an Italian family, I was keen to learn to speak the language. It was important because the Italian language trumped English in any conversation round the dinner table. The rule seemed to be that if you were speaking English, you could be cut across if someone had something to say in Italian. It was also acceptable to talk about you in Italian, in front of you, safe in the knowledge that you couldn't understand.

I had been going for lessons at the Italian Consulate for several months before Nina was born, and resumed them a few weeks after. To do so, I drove across the city to drop Nina at her Italian grandparents' before heading into the city centre for my lesson.

One evening, I was exhausted and dropped Nina with her *nonno* and *nonna* then, giving the Italian lesson a wide berth, I drove straight home, back across the city, and collapsed into bed fully clothed. The blissful memory of my head sinking into the pillow and the feel of the cool cotton duvet being tucked under my chin, knowing that nobody would disturb me for an hour, was glorious and remains unforgettable.

Upon returning to pick Nina up, I omitted to mention that instead of conjugating verbs in *passato prossimo* or practising ordering yet another *café con latte e zucchero, per favore*, I had been sunk in a deep, dreamless sleep.

Looking back, that one act of giving up and going back to bed was one of the most sensible things I did in those first frantic, difficult months.

Hold Fast

I was not good at looking after myself. I probably did not even know what my needs were, let alone how to vocalise them.

My mother-in-law was kind, but she must have forgotten the intense exhaustion of early motherhood. 'It'll be fine in another three months,' she would say with a smile, seemingly unaware that in saying 'in another three months', she may as well have been saying 'in another million years'. She would pat the sofa cushions and tell me, 'Just put your head back and shut your eyes for a minute or two.' Then she would sit down opposite me and watch me, willing me to relax. But shutting my eyes 'for a minute or two' was not enough when what I needed was twelve hours of deep unconsciousness. To close my eyes and begin to doze for a few seconds only to then be dragged back to reality was to compound the torture of sleep deprivation.

Occasionally, I would relax by plunging into one of my pre-baby creative projects – painting furniture, stripping chests of drawers, decorating surfaces in a frenzy of decoupage, with Nina watching from her bouncy chair. 'You don't need to do that!' exclaimed my mother-in-law, thinking it was the creative projects that were wearing me out, rather than it being the painting, cutting glueing and crafting that were keeping me going.

Six

Growing up in the Lancashire countryside, one of the highlights of the year was the Whit Monday parade in the nearby town of Garstang. Our village, Winmarleigh, got to choose the Festival Queen every eleven years; I happened to be the right age at the right time, and my name was drawn out of the hat.

My mother spent weeks making a white lacy dress, all puffed sleeves, gathers and frills, and I loved it.

'She'll not have one as fancy as that when she gets wed,' said my grandad.

The village mothers came to our farm to make mounds of white crepe-paper flowers to decorate the canopy I would walk under. This canopy would be manoeuvred by four pageboys wearing brown trousers and waistcoats and followed by a retinue of six attendants dressed in peach-coloured gowns – this *was* the seventies, after all.

To watch the parade, Dad got a new handmade suit, a once-in-a-decade event usually reserved for weddings. I can't remember if this was the silver-grey suit, or the dark grey herringbone or the brown check, but it was 1974 so it was probably the brown check. The little tailor came out to the farm with his tape measure round his neck and swatches of material with matching satin linings. He'd already made Dad a black suit with shiny lapels for ballroom dancing, and a few years later would make him a blazer for a cruise on the *QE2* that never happened, so, yes, this time it was most likely the seventies brown check.

Every time the tailor came, Dad was the same measurements as the day he'd got married: 'a shade under six feet tall', eleven stones and with the arms of a goalkeeper. Always keen for life to imitate art, I decided the tiny tailor looked like Beatrix Potter's *The Tailor of Gloucester* – especially when my mother remarked that in his workshop, he would sew the suit sitting cross-legged.

We all gathered round to help Dad choose the material, but obviously we knew Mum would have the final word.

The night before the parade, I went to the ladies' hair salon, Top Knott, to have a headful of spiky curlers put in which, after I sat under the dryer for half an hour, were left in overnight. I had a sleepless night trying to doze off, face planted into the pillow, wearing what amounted to a medieval torture device.

I was unaccustomed to all this fuss and preparation; I had never felt so important and *involved* in anything in my life. Church confirmation the year before had been a big event involving a magnificent buffet in the farmhouse, a new bible, a prayer book and a little gold cross, but other than that, confirmation had only necessitated getting a new white skirt and blouse and the vicar's wife tying what looked like a tea towel on my head.

Now, as festival queen, I had a *crown*.

I was crowned on a wooden platform beside Garstang Market Cross, in front of the Royal Oak pub, where the whole marketplace was packed with spectators. I read a speech of thanks my mother had written in her clear cursive handwriting in an old exercise book.

'I would like to thank the committee…'

Unfortunately, I had never used a microphone before and kept waiting for the echo to die away before resuming my speech. For a shy introvert, it was a bizarre experience to hear my voice slowly bouncing away down the high street.

My big sister, Elizabeth, grinning at me from the front row of the crowd, later told me gleefully that I had sounded like Colin

Six

Crompton, the spoof chairman of the fictional *Wheeltappers and Shunters Social Club*. This was a popular programme on Granada television at the time and Colin was famous for his broad Lancashire accent and his gormless expression and delivery: 'I. Would. Like. To. Thank. The commi-taaay.'

Not that I would have noticed or thought there was anything wrong with Colin Crompton's accent, because as far as I was concerned, Lancashire folk were the only ones in the country who *didn't* have an accent, but I was mortified that in my big moment, I had sounded daft.

After the parade, we went for sandwiches and cake in the council offices, and then on to the fairground field where I wore my crown and regal cape and presented the schools' netball trophy to the winning captain, who pretended to curtsey: 'Thank you, Yer Maj-es-ti'.

The following Wednesday, Mum took me to the newsagent to get first sight of that week's *Garstang Courier*. The front page was filled with a photograph of me looking bewildered at the market cross, with the headline 'CATHERINE THE GREAT'. '"She's great!" That was the general opinion of charming Catherine Simpson...'

My mother laughed with delight. I can still hear the sound. Despite my gaffe with the microphone, I had apparently got something right. I had done something good enough – I had looked pretty in a fancy frock – no matter that it was something that took no skill on my part and had necessitated only the pulling of my name out of a hat.

My mother gathered an armful of *Couriers* '...One for Grandma...one for Aunty Margaret...one for Aunty Brenda ...two for making scrapbooks...one for me, one for you.' I basked in the knowledge that – and this was no small achievement – I had made my mother proud.

Nearly fifty years later, that *Courier* front page still hangs on my bathroom wall.

With the Whit festival being such a childhood highlight, I had looked forward to sharing it with my own children. Nina was only two months old when the first one rolled around, but full of nostalgia for the ghosts of Whitsuntide past, I headed the 170 miles south from Edinburgh to join in. Whit Monday was a working day in Scotland, so I drove down without Cello, hoping for the best.

I stood with old school friends, Carole and Hilary, in the carpark of the Royal Oak, the pub where we'd done most of our underage drinking a lifetime earlier. In that former life, I had at times been a bit feral: aged fifteen, drinking spirits barefoot in the pub wearing my school uniform.

This was the pub car park where sixteen-year-old Carole and I had fallen over drunk during a previous Whit Monday Festival, and I had learned that friendship was someone pulling your hair out of your face when you threw up. That same Whit Monday, we had slumped in the Royal Oak doorway, worse for wear, only to see the headmaster's tanned, hairy ankles and Jesus sandals walk past as he headed into the bar for a drink of his own. 'Hello, girls!' he said, without breaking his stride.

Whit Monday was like that in Garstang – normal rules did not apply.

And now here I was, excited to see the festivities as an adult, a mother, with a gorgeous baby wearing a yellow spotty suit and a floppy broderie anglaise sun hat.

The parade of revving tractors pulling decorated floats full of fancy-dressed children headed towards us, followed by the marching pipe band led by the magnificent pipe major wearing a bearskin and carrying a mace, then the brass bands, the

Six

tumblers, the bucket shakers, and the festival queens from far and wide, all coming our way as the crowd clapped and cheered and whistled.

I hadn't been back for the festival for some years, but the town could still put on a heck of a show.

But as the parade began to get into its stride, the dream crumbled because Nina began to scream and writhe in my arms and would not be calmed. I realised with a sinking heart that in these chaotically loud and never-before-experienced circumstances, surrounded by this jostling crowd, I didn't know how to calm her – and there wasn't a cat in hell's chance of the dangling her over my arm like the Queen's handbag thing working either.

What had I been thinking, bringing her here to this busy, loud place on my own?

I fled to a nearby café, trying to smile and exchange pleasantries with familiar faces as I went.

'Hi, hi….Yes, good thank you…Yes, she's fine, fine…Good to see you…Yes, thanks, fine, fine…'

But once inside the café, still she screamed. I took refuge in the café toilet where she immediately calmed down. Faintly, I could still hear the brass bands and the cheers of the crowd as I stood between the loo and the door in the tiny space feeling isolated and alone, except for this beautiful baby with the shock of dark hair, a baby who was now peaceful, watching me with her big brown eyes, now we were alone in a toilet cubicle.

I looked at her and thought, is this the way it's going to be? Is the world too frightening for you? Is it just you and me, babe? Just you and me?

I have always enjoyed solitude, and have never been frightened of being on my own, but isolation – when I am not in control of my aloneness – is a very different thing indeed.

Seven

Waterstones on Edinburgh's Princes Street became a bolthole on a Sunday afternoon. It was somewhere I could go alone, leaving the baby with Cello and his parents, Rosa and Giuseppe, in their tiny flat for a couple of hours. They would sit around the gas fire, under the print of Raphael's Madonna and Child, and between the gilt-framed Mary of the Sacred Heart and wood-framed The Holy Family. All eyes were either on Nina, or on the Seria A Italian football *Golaccio!!!* showing on the television, which was balanced on the *cristaliere* full of glasses and ancient bottles of cherry brandy.

Every week, we had Sunday lunch of meatballs and pasta made by Rosa in a kitchenette not much bigger than a wardrobe but which worked because Rosa was such a tiny woman. If it wasn't the football season, her head would poke out of the kitchenette every minute or two to catch up on the *Eastenders* omnibus. She'd shake her head at what they were up to on the television – 'He's a-bad-a-man!' – fully believing it was all real no matter how many times we told her they were actors and that the Mitchell brothers weren't in fact brothers and didn't actually own a garage. 'No, he very bad!' It felt like telling a child there was no Father Christmas.

Then she'd shrug and declare that this week's pasta sauce was 'no very good' – apparently, it was all the fault of the meat or the tomatoes or the oil or the weather or her health or any number of other reasons. 'I cannae help it,' she'd say with a shrug and disappear back to the bubbling cauldron on the stove.

We ate the always delicious pasta, meatballs and salad around a table with a good view of the football. On the wall beside us was a framed photo of the family sitting round the

Seven

table eating pasta, meatballs and salad, while watching the football – a photograph taken for a newspaper article about authentic Italian cooking. Barolo was served, but Rosa claimed it was too strong for her stomach and with an 'I cannae help it', she diluted the rich red wine with a glug of Irn Bru.

Rosa and Giuseppe were entranced by Nina. Everything she did was delightful to them, and the feeling was reciprocated. Nina flung herself out of my arms as soon as she caught sight of Rosa, desperate for a cuddle, which made Rosa glow with pride. At eight months old, Nina could hold a *Mog's Family of Cats* board book and knew to turn it back when Giuseppe, with his one good arm following his stroke, kept turning it upside down. I remember the look of joy on Giuseppe's face as she again turned the book the right way round: 'Bella, Nina! She a genius!' The cliché of Italians adoring children is a cliché because it is true.

After lunch, once in Waterstones, I would walk past the tables of face-up titles, stroking the covers on the *Best New Books*, the *Waterstones Choices* and the two-for-ones. Running my hand over the patchwork of covers. I didn't know a writer. I had never knowingly met one. Who were these people who lived in stories and created these worlds?

As well as becoming a mother, I had also dreamt of becoming a writer Pre-motherhood, I had even fantasised about combining the two and writing a book while a baby kicked about on the floor, an image I now found cringeworthy in its naivety.

A work colleague, who was also a new mother, once told me she had been to the toilet that morning at the same time as brushing her teeth, at the same time as nursing her baby. It hadn't sunk in that writing a book at the same time as doing all of that might be tricky.

As for being a writer, it was the mid-nineties, and I didn't even own a computer. To say I needed one to write a book – or even a short story – would have felt delusional. Could I pretend I needed it for something else? These were pre-online shopping, pre-social media, pre-Google, pre-smartphone days. Being out of the workplace, what would be a plausible reason to have a computer? I couldn't think of one.

I tried briefly to imagine the charmed lives of these Waterstones authors, possibly living in cottages by the sea, or maybe in book-lined New Town apartments, somewhere without a pram in the hall.

I read about one woman writer who wrote fiction all morning then read a different novel in its entirety each afternoon, before having a chilled glass of wine and dinner with her writer husband, and I *marvelled*.

I couldn't daydream for long, though, on those Sunday afternoons in Waterstones because I had a different, more immediate reality to deal with. I'd make my way through the shop, up the stairs and to an alcove at the back – to the Family section. Among the books about weaning and breastfeeding and how to entertain your toddler in Edinburgh, there were titles like *Complete Baby and Children*, *What to Expect in the First Year*, *The Terrible Twos*, *The Incredible Years* and *The Common-Sense Book*. But there was another book: *Hidden Disabilities*. I would pore over the chapters on ADD, auditory attention problems, Asperger's syndrome (as it was then known), autism, dyslexia, depression, going through the alphabet of conditions, searching for clues – trying to understand my baby, trying to decode what was going on, because I knew something was.

Even though no one else was with me on this, I knew.

Seven

In those pre-Google days, information could not be instantly summoned. We had never heard of search engines, chatrooms or online communities. I'd face the shelves, my heart beating so hard I could feel the pulse in my scalp, and read a bit more each week, too frightened to buy the book and tempt fate.

I would become so firmly rooted to the spot, my heart in my mouth, my hands moulded to the book, that it became difficult to turn and face the world again.

I sensed the road diverging and I wanted to take the easier route – the easier one for me and the easier one for my child. I wanted to head down the road most travelled. I wanted to face the same challenges as the other mothers, and for my child to face the same challenges as the other children, but I felt a stone-cold fear in the pit of my stomach that Nina and I were already lost, stumbling alone down the road less travelled, and nobody seemed to have noticed but me.

Or maybe they had. An old school friend recalls seeing me at this time – stressed, exhausted and overwhelmed, and said, 'You looked *blue.*'

I was the first of my circle of friends to have a baby and the excitement was high at the novelty of us suddenly not being the youngest generation. Friends willingly cuddled Nina and gave her a bottle of milk. One very brave (young and childfree) couple took her for a walk to the park, and my gratitude at being given an hour's peace was off the scale. 'Can I pack you a picnic?' I asked. 'Would you like to take a bottle of wine, perhaps?' I was so grateful for the opportunity to crash out on the sofa that I almost wept.

But sharing just how overwhelmed I felt was impossible. It was as though I had jumped ship – from childless to the mothership, the ship of mothers – and I was on a very different course to all my child-free friends. I could smile and wave at them as our lives sped in opposite directions but in many ways, we were beyond communication.

And yet, I didn't want to be the one among my friendship group to change everything. I didn't want to be the one who had reset the rules of friendship; I wanted my old friendships to stay the same. I wanted us to share the same jokes and the same ways of enjoying ourselves, but as I poured over hidden disability books, I wondered if that was possible.

These were friendships I'd had since high school, these were the friends with whom I had collected my O level results, then A Level results; friends who had been in the car on those first shaky drives after passing our tests; friends with whom I had celebrated first loves, engagements, first homes and weddings. We had always felt like we were on the cusp of life together – and now real life had exploded in the form of this baby that dominated our conversations and my entire existence. It is testament to those early friendships that they are still intact more than thirty years later, babies notwithstanding.

In 1995, I would wake up each morning thinking, *maybe today. Maybe today will be the day it will be different, maybe today will be the day I can do this right, and things will fall into place. Maybe today I will be a good mother with a contented baby.* But it never was today.

Sometimes, if I had a couple of free hours on a Sunday afternoon as Cello watched football with his family and his mum fussed over Nina, instead of going to read books in a frenzy about hidden disabilities in Waterstones, I would sit in a café and the time would pass with me in a daze biting my fingers, each one, until I had made them sore, palms sweating, as my coffee turned cold and undrinkable beside me.

Seven

I look back through the early photograph albums now and see pictures of a serene sleeping baby; a curious, interested baby; a happy, smiling baby. I see Nina with wide gummy smiles laughing at the cat or in her bouncing chair or splashing in water and her whole face lighting up with joy – because of course, you only take a photograph when things are going well. On days when you've spent all morning mouleing sweet potato, bathing the baby and dressing them in clean clothes, for the baby to then be sick and immediately be dirty and hungry again, and with your hours of work having come to nothing, you don't get the camera out.

Certainly, one thing Nina was not was an FLK. My sister Elizabeth, a midwife, told me that new babies who looked strange or not quite 'normal' were referred to as FLKs – Funny Looking Kids. I took this as a joke at first, but apparently FLKs were a real thing in paediatric circles. Nina with her dark brown eyes and curls was not that – whatever was causing her difficulties was not detectable by the naked eye.

Usually, I am smiling in the photographs too. I didn't come across the term 'smiling depression' until years later, but as soon as I did, I recognised it. As a new mother, I was overwhelmed and struggling on the inside but masking it with what I hoped was a show of competence and happiness on the outside. I was terrified by the lack of control in this new life and about the lack of certainty of sleep. I was devasted that I was failing in the thing I had looked forward to most – making my child happy. It was impossible to talk about how I felt because of my fear of failure, the fear of not achieving the high standards of happiness I had set myself. There didn't seem room for my depression.

Cello was working seventy hours a week as a journalist in an all-encompassing job. The newsroom thought nothing of phoning from London at four o'clock in the morning to discuss a story, or sometimes just to say 'Right, let's call it a day,' waking us all up in the process. His mobile phone always lay beside his plate at the dining table, usually ringing more than once during dinner. He'd eat while he talked, until he had finished his meal, at which point he would return to his attic office mouthing, 'I'd better go', with an apologetic gesture towards the dirty pots.

One day, the Solicitor General phoned on the home line, responding to Cello's request for a briefing. My hands were full, I was exhausted and stretched too far, and between frying the sausages, mashing the tatties and nursing the baby, I answered the phone. Upon being told it was the Solicitor General, I said, 'Cello's in his office. When you get hold of him, can you tell him his tea's ready?' To which the Solicitor General responded with a nervous laugh.

Cello worked on Saturdays, when it was particularly hard for me to fill the days as everyone else was busy doing 'family stuff'. As Nina grew older, soft play areas became unlikely places of refuge (or at least places of desperate escape), especially on cold, wet days. They had harsh synthetic lighting and a sensation of being trapped deep underground in some 'child-friendly' hellscape of garish colours echoing with the sounds of piped musak, the unearthly screams of children buried alive beneath plastic balls, and the wails of a child being smashed in the face by another child's elbow or knee.

Soft play areas had delightful-sounding names like The Happy Castle or The Funky Forest, but delightful they were not. They were miserable places where energy levels were kept up by consuming the range of sugary snacks on offer – which, if you were lucky, were served by a human being and not a machine. Soft play was where your child's mouth and

Seven

tongue were stained blue from consuming Brain Lickers – rotating golf balls set into bottles of blue juice – or slurping neon slushies optimistically labelled 'raspberry'.

One day, there was a spat between Nina and another child in the dark depths of the Happy Castle. I didn't see what happened, but I noticed the other mother looking upset. I extracted Nina and went back to say that I hoped all was well to the other mother and child. The mother was crying and said angrily, 'He has a diagnosis! He has a diagnosis! Why does nobody understand?' Nina did not have a diagnosis at that time, so I felt a fraud, but I murmured, 'Oh, I think I do understand. I do understand.'

Soft play areas were places that made me consider my life choices. This was not what motherhood had promised. This was not a warm home with a warm kitchen, with warm baking and a warm baby, and a lot of smiling… This was the opposite of that. This was surely not part of the same experience, on the same planet as the mothers who were mouleing paw paw, sweet potato and mango as though their lives depended on it, but on many days, I simply didn't have the energy to do anything else. Sometimes, after another sleepless night, getting out of the house at all was the most I could aspire to, and on those days the soft play was where we often washed up.

One day, as I slumped in my chair at the soft play centre, the owner poked his head round the corner, looked at me and said, 'Oh, it's you again.'

Sometimes, it wasn't the soft play but the play park in Edinburgh near Rosa's flat that offered somewhere to go, the same play park my husband had played in as a boy – a play park with no grass, with rough stony tarmac, graffiti to the left of me, graffiti to the right, and depressed-looking refugees from the Bosnian war sitting silent vigil on the benches.

Hold Fast

I hated going, and my memories of the place are not happy. I wondered while writing this whether that play park could have been as depressing as I remembered it, or were my memories tainted by my feelings of failure at the time?

I went back to look – twenty-odd years since I was last there with small children.

The street is still lined with mature sycamore, the elegant four-storey Victorian tenements still overlook the park, but the park itself has had a facelift. A sign announces that a group of local people are now dedicated to transforming the park into a 'vibrant and well-used community service'. A sign headed 'Spot it: Birds and Mammals' details the wildlife there – modest stuff like robins, blackbirds, blue tits, wood pigeons and black-headed gulls. But modest or not, this is wildlife I never imagined when I was here twenty years ago. The graffiti has been painted over and turned into a mural, which for some reason depicts creatures more exotic than blue tits and blackbirds – a tiger, a toucan and an electric blue butterfly amid sprayed neon monstera and palm fronds. The squeaky, rusted swings have morphed into sturdy wooden play equipment that looks as though it has just been constructed by lumberjacks from freshly hewn trees.

This is the same park but not the same park. The park has changed – but so have I; I am now no longer viewing it through a lens of stress and loneliness, and the atmosphere now seems benign and welcoming, not hostile and toxic.

I ask both daughters what they remember about going to this park. Lara's answer comes straight back: 'Nada, sorry,' but Nina has stronger memories of swinging 'stupid high' on the swings, of the red and yellow helter skelter, of singing *See Saw, Margery Daw*, and of 'chasing pigeons until I tasted blood'. Different memories – or no memories at all – from the same place at the same time.

Seven

Memories are strange things. I have strong memories from when I was two years old: white spots on my mother's red dress, the gleam on the polished dining table, the smell of the aromatic plant by the front door of my grandmother's farmhouse. I have very clear memories of the birth of my little sister when I was just three. Maybe this is why I have become a memoir writer. Nina has equally strong memories, but Lara, before the age of seven: nada. All those holidays, all those adventures, stories, games have apparently left no trace.

When Nina was a baby, my birth family was far away, and Cello was out working all day. My father-in-law had a stroke while I was pregnant with Nina and could no longer drive himself and my non-driving mother-in-law from the other side of the city, so Nina and I spent a lot of time on our own. With the failure of the mother and toddler groups and my family being a long way away, ill or indisposed, my support system was sparse.

I had no desire to make new mother friends anyway, because I had begun to prefer being alone with Nina rather than mixing with strangers.

This was very different from the environment in which I had been raised – a 200-acre dairy farm in a village inhabited by farming aunts and uncles, and other farming families, all of whom we knew.

Growing up in Lancashire, there were relatives and family friends everywhere. My dad knew people's pedigrees two or three generations back, including which land they and their families had farmed. He loved to tell you 'She was a Colli'son afore she was married…Her mother was a…' He'd wrinkle his brow and shake his head. 'What-do-you-call-em?…They used to farm at…at…', and he'd scratch his head again and try to dredge up names and places from the past.

Hold Fast

We used to gather at my grandma and grandad's farm every Sunday, dozens of us: cousins, aunts, uncles, great aunts, great uncles, people we called 'uncle' but were not.

My mother was never more than a few minutes' car ride away from her own parents or sisters, who both had children of their own, whereas I had ended up 170 miles from my roots, and Nina and I were alone a lot of the time as Cello kept his nose to the journalistic grindstone. They say it takes a village to raise a child, but at the very least, it takes several pairs of hands.

However, I had no regrets about leaving my home village in Lancashire because I had fallen in love with Edinburgh at first sight.

Nina was born five years after I headed up to Scotland to meet Cello for the first time since we'd studied journalism together in Preston We had last set eyes on each other in a sunny Preston beer garden on the last day of term in 1988 – sitting at a picnic bench on what was in effect a bit of wasteland outside the pub, squinting into the sun as the sound of Depeche Mode's *New Life* floated out of the pub's back door.

Photos had been taken that afternoon that showed us leaning towards each other, heads together, looking happy, with a sun-blurred orange halo around my eighties perm. In the following months, there had been a tentative telephone call and a couple of letters – actual handwritten letters – that I remember sitting on a park bench to open and read:

Dear Cath, I've been missing your wit, charm and good looks so I thought I would write you a letter...Once I've got my own place I'd love to have you here for the weekend...You said you'd never been to Edinburgh...You might like to meet up? Then again, you might not. Let me know.

Then a year later, my first trip to Cello's home city of Edinburgh.

Seven

I drove, up to Scotland – the first time north of the border since my childhood caravan holiday – and a friend, Cath, who had also been on the journalism course with us, 'navigated'. We were ostensibly going for a weekend in Edinburgh, but I was also going to find out what would happen if Cello and I were in the same town again.

Cello had given us terrible directions – just a series of towns we may or may not pass through. These were pre-satnav days – although they *were* post-map days, so there was really no excuse. Nevertheless, we zig-zagged our way up through northern England and Scottish border towns, not even realising we had arrived in the capital until I glanced up to my right and had a flashback to a biscuit tin lid of old and realised I was gazing up at Edinburgh Castle.

There it was, emerging from Castle Rock, a magnificent, brooding silhouette overlooking the spectacular layered, Gothic, spired, turreted, crowned, domed, skyline of the Old Town, which in turn overlooked the lush green of Princes Street Gardens.

And that was it: I was in love.

Having met in a town of red-brick Victorian terraces where we drank Boddingtons beer in pubs with names like The Lamb and Packet, Cello and I were now in a city of Georgian sandstone tenements where we drank 80 Shilling and Laphroaig in pubs with names like The Jinglin' Geordie.

I fell in love with Cello too, of course, but Edinburgh: what a bonus.

At five months old, Nina was the perfect size to cuddle as I danced around the living room of our flat to an Early Learning Centre version of *Puff the Magic Dragon*. This was a song that had broken my heart as a child because I thought it was about the death of a dragon, rather than the growing up of a little boy. Merely the name of the mythical place of Honah Lee could still bring tears to my eyes, as I wrapped my arms around Nina and kissed the top of her head. I would sway to and fro, staring out of the bay window at the cars backing up from the traffic lights at Morningside Station, and at the off licence where I had bought the bottle of Moët and Chandon when I discovered I was pregnant with Nina.

Nina loved to be cuddled while we danced, in a way she never had when she was being breastfed.

I'd break away from the view and dance and swoop and twirl Nina around the room, and the opening line from Sylvia Plath's poem *Morning Song* would go around in my head. I'd imagine that my love for Nina was setting her going like the fat, gold watch of Plath's poem.

I squeezed her luscious fat limbs, and I knew it to be true, Sylvia was right. Love had set her going like a fat, gold watch. I sang and kissed her curls and tried to soothe her unspeakable fears of the world, of the out-there and the faraway, or sometimes her fears of the world right here and the overwhelmingly too-near.

However difficult each day was, I never doubted that I loved Nina and Nina loved me.

Eight

Cello interviewed a woman who had survived a car crash that had killed her husband and teenaged children, and in which she too had been expected to die. She was nursed back to health by nuns, and she put her recovery down to St Jude, the patron saint of lost causes. She became very religious, and following Cello's interview with her she became evangelical with us and began sending us many leaflets and books about God and love. One of these books got put in the bathroom and one day, with no other books accessible, I reached for it as I soaked in the bath. It was called *Unconditional Love* by Ed and Deb Shapiro.

Unconditional love was not a term I had previously encountered, but being the sort of person who would read the back of the cereal packet if all else failed, I opened the book and read the first page: 'Love is not love if it is bound by conditions…' It went on, 'love is non-judgemental, fearless, boundless, all embracing'.

Those words arrested me. I read them again, and as I lay there, soap bubbles popping and crackling in my ears, I recognised a description of how I loved my children; love without conditions attached, no strings, love come what may.

I also had the sobering realisation that this was not the kind of love I had received as a child. Strict terms and conditions had applied to my mother's affections. These T&Cs were not written down in any small print, they were not stipulated in any contract; they were unspoken, but they were there. They stipulated that I must be top of the class, I must always get ten out of ten, but that I must never be a nuisance, that I must not get under her feet, that I must STOP GETTING ON

HER NERVES, and that I must NEVER show her up, but that I must make her proud by BEING THE BEST in some unspecified way.

I have never been afraid to demonstrate to my children that I love them, nor am I hesitant to tell them so, which is perhaps odd as outward displays of affection in my birth family were thin on the ground, and the words 'I love you' never spoken.

In struggling to cope with Nina as a baby, I felt I was letting her down. I looked at other new mothers and wondered how they were succeeding and making it look so easy. Everywhere, there seemed to be placid mothers with placid babies – or maybe I just wasn't seeing behind their masks. There was certainly nothing placid or peaceful about my life and I was the most conscientious person I knew. If they weren't struggling, why was I?

I couldn't settle Nina; often, I couldn't calm or soothe her at all. If I thought she was in pain, I'd give her Calpol, which she'd spit out, and it would run gloopy and sticky into the folds of her neck, and she'd get hot and angry and scream even more. I was so tired, it became hard to tell what was real. We were exhausted. I once woke up with my feet on the floor and my head on the pillow and I didn't know if I'd fallen asleep getting out or getting back in.

It was as though Nina felt she did not fit into this world. The world was not Nina-shaped, and she was obliged to fight everything in it. I knew the theory about getting up, getting out of the house, fresh air, sleep when the baby sleeps, get a good routine, but it was impossible to live by. I didn't have the energy or the wherewithal to even begin. I was at exhaustion point.

Eight

When Nina was eight months old, Cello won a Journalist of the Year award, and we spent his prize money on a weekend in Stratford-upon-Avon. Looking back, I think this choice of location must have been an attempt to recreate a pre-baby reality when we had time for culture that wasn't baby-centred.

Meanwhile, Nina went for her first holiday with my parents on their Lancashire dairy farm.

I had not grasped the idea of light-touch delegation, so lengthy lists of instructions – written by me in large superclear letters in red felt pen – were left with my mother so that I could micro-manage from afar. Feeding schedules: *1 oz of baby rice must be added to 8 oz. of milk*…Sleep routines: *give bottle in dark, then leave room immediately*…Bathing requirements, soothing suggestions, *give Calpol for teeth*…as though my mother had never cared for a baby before.

She had, of course, but not this baby.

We stayed in a hotel boasting 'acres of beautiful parkland… some once owned by William Shakespeare'. A hotel that described itself as having 'old world charm and every modern luxury…' Unfortunately, it was also a hotel that had staff who got their wires crossed and who phoned us at seven o'clock on the Saturday morning: 'It's the early morning call you requested!'

'No, no…we really didn't…'

We wandered dazed and white-faced around the formal Tudor knot garden, which was trimmed and clipped to symmetrical perfection, going through the motions of a young couple on holiday. Trying to be 'normal' – forgetting that our old normal had disappeared and we had not yet reworked life into anything resembling a new normal. We tried to keep awake throughout performances of *Romeo and Juliet* and *The Tempest*, unwilling to give up on our idea of what a perfect life should be.

'A perfect life' – a fiction created for whose benefit? Not ours. The idealisation of parenthood – motherhood – was totally undermining. When did the concept of being a 'good enough' parent arise? Not then, not for me at least; possibly not for another decade or two.

When we got back to the farm, we realised my mother had misunderstood my detailed and comprehensive instructions (possibly because they were too detailed and too comprehensive) and had added 8oz of baby rice to each 8oz of formula milk – the mystery being how had Nina managed to suck this porridge out of the bottle at all. But, as it happens, Nina seemed content, so did Mum, and the world had not ended.

Nina was frightened of things I couldn't see. She often didn't answer to her name or appear to hear me when I tried to reassure her.

She loved books, and from eighteen months started to write a rudimentary alphabet. 'Have you got her *flashcards?*' demanded a friend accusingly, seeing the cards of upper- and lower-case letters on Nina's little desk. I felt a moment of mortification – what kind of a mad, pushy mother was I? But then I said, well, yes, I had, as a matter of fact, but only because she loved them. I later learned about hyperlexia – the intense early interest in letters and words and the ability to decode them at a very young age – but at the time I was happy to go with Giuseppe's opinion: 'Bella, Nina! She a genius!'

On Nina's first birthday, she sat in her highchair at her party chewing on her favourite plastic dwarf – Doc, the self-appointed leader of the seven dwarves, who she would not relinquish and who therefore had to be guarded like a crown jewel. I had begun to think of Nina as a ticking time bomb

Eight

– *Danger UXB* – and we wondered if we would get through this family party without an explosion.

There were many potential detonators: the sight of an unwrapped present – was it the sound of ripping paper, the unknown contents of the package, the unpredictable nature of a surprise present, or something else? We didn't know. Or it could be a balloon that might pop, a strange face looming too close, or a voice too loud. I look back now and wonder who we were having this party for. Nina didn't want a party: all she wanted was us and Doc. Again, I was doing it because it was, apparently, the thing to do.

By the time her second birthday rolled around, I was bone tired and I didn't organise a party. Instead, we went to see Rosa and Giuseppe and had a Cadbury's chocolate roll with two candles stuck in it, and Nina was just as happy. By now, Doc had been replaced by a pet aubergine – Audrey Jean – that she took everywhere. She put it to sleep wrapped in a blanket in the cat's bed.

I dutifully took her along to other children's parties where we played alone. I would push her on the swing while the other mums drank warm white wine on the patio or gossiped in the kitchen. And as the other kids raced round on trikes or played some rough and tumble game, I would remain pushing Nina on the swing. Backwards and forwards, backwards and forwards; together, me and her, watching the rest of the world from a distance.

I was nothing if not persistent with the dire mother and baby groups, including one where mothers sat on the floor in a circle holding their toddlers on their knees to sing songs. 'Do the actions!' We were ordered. 'Join in!' Uninvited, Nina decided to sit in the middle of the circle, then another child crawled to join her, then another, until it became clear that all hell was breaking loose, and before long *all the babies would be in the middle. No!* I was told. *This is Not Allowed! No babies in the circle! Every mum must toe the line and take their child onto their knee!*

It didn't do in this environment to be different in even the most innocuous of ways. Everything was about conformity, otherwise there would be anarchy at Tumble Teds.

We left and did not go back.

I felt increasingly disconnected from the outside world. Who even was I? Not the competent mother I had hoped to be, that was for sure.

I had been away from the work environment a relatively short time, but the world outside was changing fast. Meanwhile, I did not even have an email account, I had still never owned a personal computer, and social media and smartphones did not yet exist. By 1996, I felt that technology was disappearing beyond my reach, leaving me behind. I had left work willingly, but as technology moved into the future, I felt marooned in the past, and it was hard to imagine I would ever make it back to the world of work and offices, jargon, in-jokes and adults in lanyards. Lanyards? Where had they come from? Suddenly in the nineties, everyone who was anyone wore a lanyard to give them access to an inaccessible grown-up world.

My skills were out of date, I had no contacts, and no one to even write me a reference. I was cut adrift – but this was all beside the point because no one else could care for Nina like I could, even if I'd been able to find work. She needed me and she loved me. I needed to be with her. She smiled at Cello and obviously loved him too, but she was especially close to me. To try to explain Nina to any potential childminder was beyond me. She was far too complicated and the challenges far too

Eight

subtle – and, although I got it wrong a lot, she still needed me more than she needed anyone else, and I understood her better than anyone else.

I felt as though I was Nina's translator, her interface with the world – a feeling that persisted for many years. At home with Nina, I was in great demand, whereas in the outside world, I was fast becoming a redundant non-person.

One morning, I was sitting stock still at the kitchen table, like the bunny without the Duracell battery; drained, flat, finished. I felt dissociated from the world around me, fuzzy-headed, distanced from reality.

'You need to get to the doctor,' said Cello, with slight panic in his voice.

The doctor ran through a list of questions: *Was I having trouble sleeping? Was I finding it hard to concentrate? Had my appetite been affected?* The list went on, until he asked if I had had thoughts of suicide. This question made me snap to attention and I told him honestly that I had not. He put me on anti-depressants and recommended a short course of therapy.

The therapy consisted of me and the therapist – a middle-aged woman who either didn't have a personality or who kept it well hidden behind her smeary glasses and cardigan – sitting in a very small room looking at each other, with sporadic embarrassed remarks from me to try to cover the silence. I think I wanted her to suggest what I could do to feel better. I wanted her to have some answers, but that mustn't have been her job. Giving me helpful suggestions was not her MO.

Maybe what I really wanted was for her to put her arm around me and tell me not to try so hard and that everything would be all right in the end – but that clearly wasn't her job either. Anyway, I wasn't used to strangers putting theirs arm around me and would probably have recoiled if she had.

Instead, we avoided each other's eye until I made a few desultory remarks about how tired I was. I think I tried to describe how my life had disappeared in a puff of smoke and been replaced with an endless succession of days in which every moment was spoken for with no wriggle room for myself. Probably the word I was looking for was 'disempowered', but I had never used that word in 1996, and certainly never spoken it out loud.

I couldn't articulate that I had lost control in the labour suite and had never regained it.

The suppressed anger I felt upon leaving that room was still there, hidden and dark, and it felt imperative that it must remain suppressed. I had grown up in an angry household, with a mother who herself had anger that simmered, and that could burst forth in frightening explosions. That must not happen to me. So, I did not mention it. Instead, the therapist and I gazed over the car park for an hour a week, for six weeks, until the therapy box had been ticked.

Fortunately, the anti-depressants were more effective and within a few weeks, there was a break in the clouds, and I caught sight of a few shafts of sunlight as they began to shine through.

Nine

When Nina was two and a half, I was pregnant again. I did not admit it, but one of my motivations for having another child was to experience motherhood as others appeared to experience it – because I was sure I had not done so, so far. And if Nina's challenges were my fault, then maybe I could get it right this time.

Before I had another baby to care for, I decided I must go to the doctor and voice my concerns that something was different about Nina. The *Hidden Disabilities* book in Waterstones had given me dribs and drabs of information but left me no nearer. It was not easy to ask for help because it was in my bones to keep quiet, say nothing, not make a fuss. I had absorbed this attitude. It had been bred into me without me trying, or wanting it to.

I did not get any support in my search for answers.

'It can't be so bad if you're having another one!' announced my mother to visitors, with an eye roll and a dry chuckle, determined not to countenance my worries. My mother's main concern about Nina was whether she could do anything new this week that my mother could show off about to her friend who also had a new grandchild.

'Can Nina say a nursery rhyme yet? X can say *Grand Old Duke of York*.' 'Does Nina know her numbers yet? X can count to five!'

My mother was a woman who cared about attainment, not effort, and had never taken on board the idea that comparison was the thief of joy.

'Lie to her,' suggested another mother. 'You live far enough away, you can tell her anything,' and I marvelled. It was so simple – and yet the thought had never occurred to me.

My sister said, 'This new baby might be exactly like Nina,' to which I replied, 'No, they won't because I will come down on them like a ton of bricks from day one.' So I obviously believed, to some degree, that our difficulties *were* the fault of my parenting, of my not having been hard enough.

But despite close family not acknowledging my difficulties – *All children have trouble sleeping, Catherine…all children get upset…all children cry a lot…it's a phase…it'll pass…* – other people, outside the family, could clearly see that I was struggling.

'What's wrong with her?' asked a mother I had only just met at a different but equally dire mother and toddler group, as Nina played alone not interacting with the other children. I did not know then about 'parallel play', where autistic children enjoy playing in the same space but not directly with other children. I tried to laugh and shrugged, 'She's fine.'

'Maybe you should go and see a psychologist?' suggested another, nursing her perfect toddler, after Nina had been inconsolable for no obvious reason. I was not grateful for these interventions. I was rendered mute by how blunt and insensitive people could be, caught off guard every time. Maybe it was all these rude people who were upsetting her – they were certainly upsetting me. Perhaps we would always be better off on our own.

Parents are naturally proud of their children and can be huge show-offs about their wonder-babies. One mother said to me, 'Our Claire wants to be a doctor when she's grown up, don't you, Claire?' Claire was three. 'Claire, come and tell Catherine what you want to be when you're grown up.' Claire edged nearer, reluctant, shy, and muttered, 'I want to be a pony.'

Instead of boasting about Nina, I seemed to spend a lot of time struggling to explain her to other people, when I didn't

Nine

understand her myself. *'She's fine, she just doesn't really like... She's not sure about... Oh, sorry about that. I think you must have taken her by surprise...'*

My husband said it didn't matter what other people said – it was none of their business. And I replied, 'That's easy for you to say when you're not the one who's there with her.'

Other people were more circumspect: 'I think Nina may be...very, very...clever.'

I tried many techniques to encourage Nina to fit in socially: coaxing, cajoling, persuading, going with the flow (what other people probably thought of as indulging her). I was constantly problem-solving and searching for solutions. I had more diplomatic skills than a top-flight United Nations envoy, but experience taught me that distraction was the most powerful tool.

Nina was very determined, and it was hard to stop her if she wanted to grab another child's toy or to pull their ponytail. I realised that if I asked her, 'Nina, where's your tummy?' she would instantly forget what she was about to do and point to her stomach. Sometimes I had to break off adult conversations to yell, 'Nina, where's your tummy?' across soft plays, parties or playgroups. I remember the frowns I got from other uncomprehending mothers. Why did this on-edge mother freak out and shout daft questions at her child across the room like that?

I had to be eagle-eyed for potential trouble – one day, I wasn't eagle-eyed enough and my stomach sank as I caught sight of a ball of blonde hair from a little girl's ponytail rolling across the playgroup mat like tumbleweed in a Western, and the little girl crying. That was one of the days we made a hasty exit.

I spent a long time pushing Nina round the charity shops in her buggy, just the two of us, buying her little toys to play with. One day, I had obviously been in one charity shop too many and she was hungry, so I dashed into a nearby café to give her the bottle I had prepared. She was panicking and furious. An old man at the next table, slumped over his cup of tea and *Daily Record*, announced to the room in general, 'You've done something to that child to make her cry like that.' I said nothing but felt like I had been slapped. Nina couldn't tolerate strangers and soon, neither could I.

The GP listened to my concerns and said, 'We need to get you some help before the new baby comes,' and he put me on a waiting list for the Sick Kids Hospital in Edinburgh to see the 'leading expert in autism in Scotland'.

Two years before I gave birth to Nina, I had graduated as a mature student with a degree in Communication Studies, and prior to that, I gained the National Council for Training of Journalists certificate for a career in journalism. But after four years of study, I decided I didn't want to be a journalist after all. Newsrooms were too ego-filled for me. Instead, I wanted to help people, and I had decided to work for a charity. Naively, I assumed that people must be nice if they worked in the voluntary sector.

An autism charity was advertising for communications staff. I didn't really know what autism was, so in those pre-Google, pre-internet days, I went to Edinburgh Central Library and asked the librarian for help, and she dug me out some reference books.

I was shocked by what I read. Not about the autism but about how in the 1940s and 50s, the mothers had been blamed for creating the autism in their children. They were labelled 'Refrigerator Mothers' and were accused of having a 'lack of maternal warmth' that caused their children's problems. These

Nine

mothers were in effect diagnosed with a 'disorder of parenting' and one researcher described them as 'defrosting just long enough to produce a child'. Some experts recommended, for the good of the child, that a 'parentectomy' should be carried out – that the parent should be cut from the child's life for good.

I had gazed around the library aghast at what I'd just read, the unfairness of it – this injustice from forty years before was terrifying and heartbreaking. However, I hoped that these attitudes had been consigned to the past, to a far-off, bygone, unenlightened age. Surely attitudes and understanding of autistic children and their parents were different in the 1990s?

We took Nina to the hospital to see 'the leading expert on autism in Scotland' when she was two and a half. She trotted round his office taking no notice of us, or him, but examining closely everything on his shelves. I tried to explain the nature of the challenges we were facing, but he laughed – literally laughed in my face – as he said, 'That child does not have autism.'

In 1997, autism was still thought of as a male condition.

'You are giving her the wrong kind of attention,' he said. 'That is what is causing the problem. You must ignore her if she has a tantrum. Just let her cry. You are creating the bad behaviour by rewarding it with attention.'

I noticed there was a book on his shelves written by the 'leading expert on autism in Scotland' himself, about 'Problem Children'. 'Ah yes,' he said, 'we should have used the phrase "children with problems", not "problem children" but we've learned a lot since then,' and he smiled indulgently and forgivingly at himself.

He agreed to see us again so we could report back on how we were getting on 'not rewarding bad behaviour with attention'.

Ignoring tantrums was to be the order of the day. We apparently needed to undo the damage we had caused by giving Nina the wrong kind of attention. He claimed we had not given her enough positive attention when she was happy and co-operative and had therefore inadvertently encouraged bad behaviour. 'Any attention is better than no attention,' chided 'the leading expert on autism in Scotland', and added, 'so, if necessary, the child will act up to get your attention.'

I left the hospital determined to follow his advice, after all he was the 'leading expert…etc', he was the person in the hospital with 'Dr' written on his door. Those were the days when I didn't realise not everyone with Dr written on his door in a hospital has a medical degree.

But something did not feel right about his advice.

Nina had been surrounded by love and positive attention from the moment she was born whether she was being good, bad or indifferent. How had we got everything so wrong? How could pouring all that love into her have been the wrong thing to do?

We left his office joining another generation of parents blamed – albeit in a different way – for causing the difficulties of our children.

A few days later, I was out shopping with Nina in the buggy when she started screaming. I was heavily pregnant and could feel the sweat prickling my back as her screams rose and she arched her body in her seat, kicking her heels and fighting with the safety straps. My hands went clammy on the buggy handle, but I had my instructions – I must ignore this tantrum. I knew she wasn't hungry or cold, she had a drink and toys to play with and she didn't appear to be ill, so ignore her I must.

Nine

I carried on walking round the shop, the picture – I hoped – of serenity and authority. I pretended to browse the shelves and yet every fibre of my being was tuned to my daughter wrestling around in her buggy.

A little old lady with a grey anorak, grey shopping bag and grey perm sidled up: 'You're not fit to be a mother leaving a child to cry like that.' I gripped the buggy handle and turned to gaze into her little grey raisin face, and something snapped. Two and a half years of frustration burst forth and I was mute no more. 'The doctor has told me to ignore her tantrums,' I said. 'The doctor! The psychologist!' My voice had risen by an octave. 'Somebody who knows *more* about this than *you do!*'

By now, I was shouting at the top of my voice. Other shoppers stopped browsing and turned towards us, frowning, curious, concerned. But the old woman was unfazed and said, 'Well, I'm glad you're not my mother,' at which I burst into loud sobs. The assistant rushed out from behind the till carrying a chair: 'Are you all right? Would you like to sit down?' She was clearly worried I might give birth there and then between the bric-a-brac and the children's books.

I plumped down on the seat, gulping and sobbing and trying to tell her the story of our visit to the psychologist, 'the leading expert on autism in Scotland' himself, no less, who had said we should…but I couldn't get it out. The young assistant looked sympathetic. 'They don't understand, some people,' she said as we both watched the Grey Lady shuffle from the shop. 'Take no notice.'

Nina was sitting quietly in her buggy now, fascinated by all the drama. Perhaps she had just been bored – if so, ever the curious child, she wasn't bored now. I pushed her back to the car, and chatted to her in a quiet voice as I strapped her in. I was acting the soothing in-control parent even as my heart was hammering in my chest and my hands were clammy and shaking. I continued talking in a calming voice partly to reassure her and partly to calm myself.

As I drove away, I passed the shop where it had happened and found myself scanning the pavement for the Grey Lady and I felt the fury rise again, like road rage, possessing me, almost blinding me. I imagined mounting the curb, pinning her against the shop front with my car bumper, or running her over. Thankfully, the Grey Lady had vanished, because in that moment I was capable of anything. I turned *Puff the Magic Dragon* up loud so Nina couldn't hear me crying all the way home.

When I described the Grey Lady event to Nina years later, she said, 'I sound every bit like the textbook definition of a psychopath. Many people would use words like "sociopath" and "narcissist" and "manipulative" for such a person.'

'You were *two and a half years old,*' I said.

I started to have a vomiting, eviscerating fantasy. Images of pulling out my guts and throwing up everything inside me, leaving me hollow and empty, kept flashing through my mind, especially when I was driving the car. My sister Elizabeth once told me the story of a monkey that was in so much pain, it pulled out its own intestines to try to find the pain and get rid of it. I couldn't stop thinking about that monkey.

I seemed to be weaving along the grey borderline between sanity and insanity.

Ten

Nina could not get to sleep, which complicated everything. We would put her to bed, but she would lie in the dark with her eyes open, apparently unable to drop off. She would still be awake hours later. 'She's not trying!' my husband would say in frustration, but as I pointed out to him, if *he* was lying in a darkened room he wouldn't have to *try* to sleep – he couldn't have stayed awake to save his life.

I asked for advice from health workers: always stick to a regular bedtime, use a night light, open the door, close the door, read a story, sing a song, stay quiet, potter about where she can hear you.

Nothing worked.

Against advice, I lay on the bed with her to help her sleep. That didn't work either. The only thing that made even a slight difference was when next door's cat decided to move in and sleep on her bed – and even then, I don't think Nina was asleep, just comforted. I prayed that the neighbours would let the cat stay, even when another neighbour wrinkled her nose and said, 'I think you've stolen that cat.'

As the months ticked by, we became increasingly exhausted and later, when it transpired that our second daughter, Lara, was a poor sleeper too, we decided to take the night in shifts. Cello would be on duty until 4am, while I slept on a camp bed in the ensuite bathroom, then from 4am I was in charge. As grim as this was, at least I knew I could get a few solid hours and I could survive on that, albeit in a state of severe jetlag.

'Have you tried a milky drink at bedtime?' suggested the health visitor with an earnest smile. I don't think people said 'No shit, Sherlock' then, but my facial expression must have said something similar.

Hold Fast

Nina had the most beautiful head of brown ringlets, and as she passed her third birthday, she had still never had a haircut and her ringlets were reaching down to her bottom. The idea of taking her to a hairdresser and having a stranger interact with her at such close quarters in an unfamiliar environment was unthinkable.

Hers was a head of hair that you saw dotted about at Italian family gatherings – lush, dark and big, a family trademark on my husband's side that I would have loved. As gorgeous as they were, though, her curls caused a problem. Getting a comb through them was impossible and as Nina was super-sensitive to pain on her scalp, it created huge stress every morning. With stress levels already high after another sleepless night, I took the easy way out and only gave her curls the most cursory brush, then left them to do their own thing. This was one of those occasions when choosing your battles seemed to be appropriate. Surely insisting on brushing her hair thoroughly everyday wasn't a battle worth fighting?

Unfortunately, 'doing their own thing' meant turning into dreadlocks. 'Look!' gasped my niece upon encountering the matts underneath the ringlets, and I felt embarrassed and neglectful. Eventually, I knew I must tackle the ever-growing dreadlocks, so Cello distracted her with a game as I sneaked behind and hurriedly chopped off handfuls with the kitchen scissors.

Dealing with Nina's hair was an ongoing challenge. In African-American Vernacular English, they have a term for this: 'tender headed'. I have hair as straight as a poker and was clueless over how to care for Nina's ringlets.

I had read about mothers taking out their frustrations on their children by over-vigorously brushing their hair and yanking it and ripping at their scalps, hurting their children under cover of taking care of them. I did not want to fall into that trap.

Ten

My own mother – practical to the last – had dealt with the hair issue by getting our long, brown, silky hair cut off. Why this was considered necessary I don't know as our hair was relatively easy to manage. 'Do you want to look like a Beatle?' she asked, as my aunt laughed. This must have been 1968 or so when The Fab Four were at their height. However, I was five years old and unfamiliar with international pop stars and their moptops – I was more familiar with the black shiny beetles that lived behind the fireplace. It is testament to my mother's powers of persuasion and my need to please that I agreed to have my hair cut like a Beatle/beetle anyway. My father was disappointed – he liked our hair long with ribbons on top – but as my mother informed him, he wasn't responsible for looking after it, so he had no say in the matter. After being given my moptop, I was still ignorant of John, Paul, George and Ringo, but could definitely see some resemblance to the odd shiny headed weevil or carpet beetle that dodged into the dark of the farmhouse skirting boards.

Leaving both my daughters' hair to grow long was another way of differentiating my childhood from my children's.

Years later, as a teenager, Nina would solve the hair issue in her own way by shaving it all off, then growing a mohawk, sometimes straightening, getting an undercut, shaving patterns in the fuzz, going elfin, urchin, blue, green and pink.

Despite the difficulties, I kept up a brave face and threw myself into giving Nina the ideal childhood I had envisaged – I took her to the Festival Theatre to see Prokofiev's ballets *Cinderella*, and *Romeo and Juliet*, during which she pirouetted in the aisles in her glittery dress and fur coat. I took her to see a pianist playing Mozart piano sonatas at the Usher Hall because she had expressed a little interest in the piano keys at home. I booked seats in the organ gallery, unaware these seats were practically on the stage facing the main auditorium. So, as the soloist played exquisite music, Nina and I stared out at two thousand serious concert goers who stared back at us, and I prayed to a God I didn't believe in to let me, and my three-year-old daughter, survive this experience without her having a tantrum or indeed making any sound at all. Maybe God was listening that day, or more likely Nina was fascinated by this new experience, because she sat quietly, listening, right through to the interval when I told her the concert was over and we slipped away.

Why did I put myself through such stress? Like I say, I was wavering between sanity and insanity.

As always with a new experience, I had bought Nina a relevant book to help her understand my pregnancy…She had been busy studying the Usborne *New Baby* book, all about Mrs Bunn going into hospital to have a new baby. Mrs Bunn already had a son, a daughter, a dog and a cat. She was tired, and her house was slightly disorganised, but she was industrious and smiled all the time – things may have been demanding but they were never *too* hard for Mrs Bunn. There were always plenty of helping hands around, and life was essentially cosy in the Bunn household.

The propaganda about motherhood starts early.

Mrs Bunn breastfed her baby, of course she did. My mother nodded in approval as Nina sat on the hearth rug and played at breastfeeding her own doll, then got her doll to breastfeed a plastic dinosaur. 'She's learning,' my mother said, nodding approvingly, despite not having been able to breastfeed herself.

I don't remember being irritated by Mrs Bunn all those years ago when I bought the book for Nina, but she irritates me now

Ten

– risible Mrs Bunn, Mrs Matronly-hair-in-a-bun, Mrs Rising-like-a-yeasty-bun, Mrs Bunn the *Happy Families* baker's wife, Mrs Bunn-in-the-kitchen-with-a-rolling-pin, Mrs Bunn-in-the-oven, Mrs Bunn the saint, the martyr, the everywoman.

Oh, do fuck off, Mrs Bunn.

When Cello was driving me to hospital as I was in labour with Lara, I was asking myself: what are we doing? We are only just learning to cope with Nina – *what are we doing?* But every contraction and bump in the road underlined it was too late to worry about that now.

I had brought a selection of bedding from home – anything to feel safer than I had the first time I gave birth. The receptionist frowned and peered over the desk as Cello dumped an armful of pillows and a quilt on the floor alongside my bag. I didn't care how daft we looked; I had vowed that I would never again feel as vulnerable as I had the first time.

I climbed onto the bed in the labour ward, and I heaved a sigh of relief. All I had to do today was give birth – besides that, I had the day off. No actual mothering to be done for a few hours: the grandparents were temporarily in charge of that. Nobody could ask me to wrangle a toddler today, nobody could ask me to solve any more unsolvable problems.

Now that I was in the labour ward, the rest of the world would have to take care of itself. All I had to do was deliver this baby, and I could do that with my head on my own pillow, and that felt luxurious.

We took Lara home the next day and I was braced for the difficulties to begin. A few days later, I lay her on the bed as I got changed and I gazed at her as she kicked her legs and stared unblinking at the ceiling, and I realised this baby was different

– this baby had been born into a world that fitted. This baby was not at odds with everything around her.

This was going to be a different journey.

I had several friends with two children who had different personalities – and usually this was put down to gender. If they were unsettled or considered difficult in some way, 'Ah, well, that's girls for you!' or if they were considered boisterous, happy-go-lucky or more loving, 'Ah, well, that's boys for you!' I obviously knew this was rubbish as I had two very different babies who were both girls.

Lara was a poor sleeper and demanded to be held when she was awake. This time, I could breastfeed and got so adept that I could breastfeed whilst wandering about the house or answering the door without breaking my stride.

'That's not an easy baby!' said friends, but she seemed easy to me.

'Let's have another one straight away,' I suggested to Cello. 'She's so easy, I could do two like this one at once.'

'No. No. No,' said Cello, turning his back to me and pulling the duvet up under his chin.

Nina, always keen to draw pictures, began to create drawings of Mummy, Daddy and Nina as she always had, but now there was an additional baby-suited figure in the frame. Day by day, this figure grew bigger and bigger, taking up more and more of the page, until this terrifying baby-monster-creature dominated the drawing completely, at which point it began to grow fangs.

An old school friend, Mary Anne, who now worked in the music industry, got in touch to say she was doing a gig in Edinburgh, and she would put me on the guest list. This was a clarion call from another world, an adult world, a cool world,

Ten

an impenetrable world of clubs, electronic dance music, late hours, and definitely no babies. I was still breastfeeding Lara and living in a rotating set of baggy jumpers and the elasticated trousers that had been my staple wardrobe when I was nine months pregnant. I had no idea what I would wear to such an event, nor how to behave if I got there.

The last time I had been dancing with Mary Anne was fifteen years earlier at the village disco where we had pogoed round our handbags (my handbag, at least). The whole world had changed since then. What *even was* dubstep?

I had no clue how to extricate myself from my domestic responsibilities to be able to go. A night at a club gig felt so far out of my reach as to be an impossibility. I couldn't go, but felt uncomfortable and embarrassed that that was the case.

A few months later, Mary Anne invited me and Carole down to London to stay in her flat. This time, I was determined to go. By then, I had ditched the elasticated trousers and lost ten pounds' baby weight. I bought a pair of black trousers, a black top and black sandals, so I could merge into the London background.

Cello couldn't take time off work so my mother and John, an old university friend of Cello's, were persuaded to come and stay to look after the children – Mum as chief cook and bottle washer, and John as Entertainments Officer.

Once in London, Carole and I noted the sophistication of Mary Anne's flat, with its glass bricks inset into the bathroom wall making it possible for people in the living room to see the blurry shape of anyone moving within. We marvelled at the worldliness of it. How edgy! This must be life in London. And we wondered whether we could be unselfconscious enough to use such a bathroom.

At Soho House, we kept checking sidelong for any celebrities

– Steve Coogan was in the other night, apparently – and we drank sea breezes: grapefruit juice, cranberry juice and vodka. Longer and colder and not as sweet as the vodka and lime cordials we used to drink at the Royal Oak when we were fifteen, but almost as good. I tried not to gasp at the prices. How much was a sea breeze? I twisted my neck to catch a glimpse of a menu upside down. *How much?* I could hear my dad's voice: 'Eee, they know how to charge, don't they?'

At a club afterwards – all bare surfaces, metal and concrete industrial chic – many sea breezes and glasses of champagne later, neither Carole nor I could be bothered to go to the bar, so we tipped some melted ice from our champagne bucket into our glasses to try to off-set the cocktails. A member of staff dashed over to let us know that that was in fact an ice bucket, clearly thinking we needed looking after, or taking in hand, or something. We laughed until we nearly slid off our plank banquette.

I felt like a correspondent from a foreign land, from a land of domesticity and babies, a land far, far away from here.

One night, Cello was out working, reporting on a story on the west coast of Scotland, something to do with Princess Diana's mother. He would not be back that night. I fed Lara and put her in her cot where she settled. Shortly after, I found Nina balanced on the side of the cot bending over to look at her. I whispered that we must leave the room or Lara might wake, whereupon Nina flung herself on the carpet and drummed her heels. In a moment of fury, desperation and exhaustion, I grabbed her hand and dragged her from the room, along the carpet, unaware that as I was leaving, the door was silently swinging shut behind me. As I crossed the threshold, the edge of the door hit Nina's head.

Ten

I still remember the sound and the painful lurch of my heart.

I was appalled and had a fleeting urge to call the social services and ask for help, although I had no idea how to actually call the social services, nor quite what help I thought they could give me.

I made sure Nina was all right and put her in bed, and went and sat on my own bed, head in hands, guilt-stricken and mortified. I thanked God we had a meeting coming up with the 'leading expert in autism in Scotland' the following week – even though so far none of his advice had helped, he was the only life raft I had to cling to.

I knew I was in trouble, struggling to cope, sinking, doing a bad job, overwhelmed, failing in the one thing I had wanted to succeed at most.

Shortly after, we received a letter from the NHS telling us that 'the leading expert, etc' was leaving the Sick Kids Hospital. No explanation was given.

Cello asked around his journalist friends who told him the doctor had been found to have pornography in his office at the hospital.

I wrote him a letter to say how glad I had been to have someone to talk to and thanking him for listening. He never replied. Looking back, I was always so pathetically grateful for any 'help', even when it did no good.

So, we were back on our own.

Eleven

Nina was clearly frustrated by the world and sometimes hurt herself by banging her head on the floor. It was hard to accept that after all the fantasies I'd had about creating the happiest family imaginable, the 'Perfect Family', the reality was that I couldn't even prevent my daughter wanting to hurt herself.

She had what were described by others as tantrums but what seemed to me to be manifestations of deep wordless distress. At other times, she reminded me of a small, terrified animal at bay. I loved her so much, and I knew she loved me, but I didn't have any answers to take away her fear.

Sometimes she would be happy in her own world and still manage to be told she'd done the wrong thing. One day, I was standing at the kitchen window watching her swinging, a look of pure joy on her face as she flew so high – a feeling I remembered from my own childhood. Meanwhile, Lara toppled off the swing beside her and fell under Nina's feet, and yet Nina was completely oblivious. If Lara stood up, she would get knocked to kingdom come by Nina's wooden swing seat.

I hammered on the window and screamed through the glass but as Lara wailed, Nina was miles away in her own world, swinging hard. By the time I got out of the back door and round the house, I was frantic and shouted at Nina, 'Did you not see her?' But of course, the answer was 'no'. There had been no badness, no malice, but without doing anything except being exhilarated by flying high on the swing, she had ended up being told she'd once again got it wrong.

It was easy for us to misunderstand each other. I would grab Nina when I was crossing the road, weaving her between parked cars, only for Nina to announce loudly, 'Mummy, stop

Eleven

pushing me into the traffic.'

My mother phoned one day to tell me, 'Elizabeth thinks Nina's problems are your fault. You're too soft.' I was flabbergasted, deeply hurt and furious.

Even loathing confrontation as I do, I couldn't let this pass. I phoned my sister to ask about this remark. She was out, but her husband spluttered, 'Liz would never say such a thing.' I decided, whether Elizabeth had said it or not, it had obviously been my mother's opinion, but she hadn't had the courage to say so outright.

Nina was excited about starting school – delighted with the uniform and the plaits and the idea of being more grown up. Sadly, the shine soon wore off and before long, she was deeply unhappy.

We took her out of school for a week in her first year so we could go on holiday to Puerto Pollensa in Majorca. Those were the days when it was not considered a criminal offence to do so and there were no fines, or at least if there were, we didn't know, and the school never said. We felt very brave relocating Nina for a week, taking her away from all that was familiar at home, but because Nina found school so stressful, it was also a relief.

As usual, I was determined to put 100 per cent into it. Cello walked up and down the sea front with a sleeping Lara in a backpack as I sculpted huge reclining mermaids out of sand on the beach, and Nina and I decorated them with stones and shells. I remember seeing another parent eyeing me a little puzzled, from under the brim of his sunhat, as he reclined on the beach, clearly thinking, *What are you doing? Calm down!* But I could not calm down. I was used to being 100 per cent on duty 100 per cent of the time, and this did not change just because we were supposed to be on holiday.

Nina often didn't respond when I tried to talk to her. It was a puzzle: could she not hear me, was she unable to understand me, or was she choosing to ignore me? The doctor sent her for a hearing test, but her hearing was perfect. This didn't surprise me because sometimes she followed my instructions to the letter. 'Jump up!' I'd said to her as she sat on the toilet, and I was bending over to help pull her trousers up. And jump she did. Literally. Inadvertently headbutting me so hard in the mouth that my front tooth went numb.

I remember watching her pottering around while the World Cup tournament in France played on the television in the background. She was three years old, and I was dying to chat with her, but it wasn't possible. I thought, 'Come what may, by the time the next World Cup is on, Nina will be seven years old, and I will definitely be able to chat with her and really get to know how she feels about things and why.'

But four years later, when the tournament was back on the television, this time in Japan and South Korea, our ability to communicate remained complicated and difficult, and at times still felt impossible. It is difficult to describe exactly why, but it was something to do with Nina being so lost in thought that any interruption was a frustrating intrusion into her thought processes and made her angry. When she *did* engage in conversation, it could be glorious. One day, as we drove past a church, I pointed out its attractive tower, to which she replied, 'Yes, and just think how beautiful it would be with a ribbon tied round it.'

The children of course were changing as subtly and surely as a sky at dawn. Small changes, glimpses of the people they would become, and I was fascinated and intrigued. Every time Nina did something new and unexpected, I thought, *This is the best stage. This is the best stage now she can smile…now she*

Eleven

can walk…now she can talk…now she can write… Each phase seemed more rewarding than the last, and *none* of them as terrifying as a newborn baby.

By age seven, Nina did not want to go to school. The children's self-imposed rules of socialising had changed – boys were not allowed to play with the girls anymore, and vice versa, and among the group of girls there were cliques, none of which Nina belonged to. She did not connect with the girls. Despite playing make-believe games at home about wizards or inspired by video games with a male friend, she was embarrassed by the girls' make-believe games about 'mummies and babies' or games based on reality shows she had never seen. *Come on, guys, this is silly.*

Being profoundly lonely is Nina's defining memory of those years.

When I was at primary school, I'd had one best friend, Alex, and at that time assumed everyone had an Alex. Alex and I had walked around the playground arm in arm at every playtime. She shared her strawberry-flavoured Pink Panther chocolate bar with me at morning break and let me use her felt pens and skipping rope – a far superior skipping rope to mine, which was not really a skipping rope at all but a length of washing line. I was never alone because I had Alex. I believed at the time that children were put on this earth in matching pairs.

Knowing Nina was alone at school created a physical pain that pierced right through me.

Leaving her there reminded me of when I was a child, and I saw a sitting hen abandon her egg. The egg was put in the warm airing cupboard on a pile of old blankets and pillowcases where I could see the chick trying to chip its way out of the shell. My mother told me not to help it, that if the chick wasn't strong enough to hatch on its own then it wasn't strong enough to survive and we must leave it to die. I heard it cheeping, telling us it was trying to get out, but gradually the cheeps faded away and the chick died in the shell.

It was a harsh lesson, and not a useful one: if something couldn't survive on its own, it must die.

Nina asked me not to make her go to school, but thinking I was doing the right thing, I insisted. I felt like a monster, and I regret it still.

At that point, primary school was doing her more harm than good – with its endless worksheets and word searches, its group work and noisy corridors and overwhelming playgrounds, Nina would have been better off at home reading books. But there was a terror on my part that if I withdrew Nina from school, *she would never fit in. She would never belong.* She would never make friends. She would never be able to face the outside world. I was clinging to the hope that we would one day, somehow, achieve the mythical 'normality'.

I didn't consider that school itself may be causing the damage that would make all these things more difficult for her in the future.

One day, I found a note in Nina's bedroom. 'Do not mak me go to school,' and when I said she must go because it was the law, there was another note: 'Never trust your mummy because your mummy could be a witch.'

She dealt with her distress in imaginative ways, including concocting magic spells to get rid of her teacher. 'How to Turn Nightmare Teachers into Cute Little Guinea Pigs. Method: get the biggest sause pan in your house (a cauldron would be good). Find three slugs, four holly berries and a packet of sugar…Throw your teacher in, and there you have it!' Followed

Eleven

by another spell to turn 'Do as You are Told Parents into Chocolate Cake.'

During the Christmas holiday, she wrote to Tony Blair at 10 Downing Street telling him she didn't want to go back to school. There must have been a lull in the workload at Number 10 over the holiday, because within days she received a reply:

Dear Nina,

The Prime Minister has asked me to write and say how disappointed he was to hear that you do not enjoy school.

Your poems about school were passed to this office by your mum, Catherine. She is obviously worried about you and cares a great deal that you should do well in your lessons.

It is very important that children go to school and work hard so that they can live a full and happy grown-up life and make their family proud of them.

Mr Blair sends his very best wishes for a happy and successful future.

Was it very important that she go to school and work hard so she could live a happy grown-up life? Was I forcing her to go to make me proud? I was certainly terrified of what would happen if she didn't go. Education seemed like a portal to a happy life, an escape, but was it a price worth paying when it made her so deeply unhappy?

Nina was not surprised to receive a reply from Tony Blair because she had previously sent a letter to the Queen during her Golden Jubilee: 'Dear Your Majesty, I hope you have a happy life,' written on a collage of a red-faced queen wearing a crown made of screwed up foil. A letter had arrived in response from a Lady-in-Waiting on a letter headed 'Buckingham Palace':

I am commanded by the Queen to write and thank you for your letter and the lovely picture you made for Her Majesty. The Queen thought it was very kind of you to send this to her, and I am to thank you very much.

Nina had been proud of that reply and had taken it to school and read it out in assembly. This time, with her reply from Tony Blair, she refused to take it. 'No, I'm not taking it. They'll know I didn't want to come back.'

From my adult perspective, Nina's primary school looked friendlier than mine had when I was a schoolgirl. We had been ruled by a humourless, inflexible, lemon-sucking headmistress of the dusty old-school who crept about in rubber-soled lace-ups and tweed skirts, spreading fear wherever she went. She had addressed each child as 'Dear' but added a sprinkle of vinegar by pursing her lips. She lived in a distant village and as she left each afternoon in her beige Austin Allegro, I had imagined her arriving home at the crypt, carefully descending the dank steps, easing herself into her coffin and slowly lowering the lid till morning.

By comparison, Nina's teachers, with their costume jewellery, bobbed hair, floaty cardis and desk drawers full of biscuits, looked benign – but that was not how Nina was experiencing it.

I invited a steady stream of little girls from her class for tea and to play after school. We had a trampoline in the garden, a swing set with a slide, and a pink hammock. One little girl gazed at the garden from the front seat of the car as we drew up and remarked 'So. You have a park.'

But during these visits, Nina would soon tire of intense one-to-one playing and drift off upstairs on her own, and I would be left making crispy cakes or gluing sparkles on a collage with the little visitor, when all I wanted to do was to collapse somewhere.

Eleven

It took me a long time to realise that I was imposing my idea of what fun was onto Nina, who clearly had a different idea of what constituted a good time. Having classmates round to do girly things like dressing up or playing with dolls would have been something I would have enjoyed as a child, and I could not stop myself trying to impose this idea of successful playing onto Nina.

Some of the girls invited her back and I was grateful, albeit anxious. Especially after one mother phoned to say that Nina had got into her daughter's bed and refused to get out, and perhaps I should go and pick her up.

Other mothers seemed to think I was a free childminder. 'Oh, I've had such a lovely time again, relaxing,' said one mum, who never reciprocated with invitations, as I dropped her child off for the umpteenth time. I had just spent the afternoon making fairy cakes with her daughter as Nina had taken refuge upstairs. Once again, I was reduced to driving home in tears. I got home and lay on the sofa, and Nina came and covered me with a blanket.

I never learned. Sometime later, I got a call from the mother of a friend of Lara's: 'Is Lara busy today?' No, I said, she was free. 'Oh, could I drop off my daughter for a few hours then?' Sometimes I wondered if because we had a big house and a big garden, life looked easy for me and that was why some mothers offered no reciprocation.

I threw big birthday parties for Nina and Lara at a trampoline centre in an old church. There were no dreaded organised games, it was free play all the way in a space vast enough for thirty children to have plenty of room. There was no pass the parcel with its unbearable suspense, nor musical chairs with its terrible unpredictability. These would have been too much for Nina and hence too much for me.

Hold Fast

The hospitality rules for Nina and Lara were simple: either invite everyone in the class or invite fewer than half the class. I couldn't bear the thought of only one or two children in the class being left out, and I was flabbergasted when I heard one mother say that her son would not invite a certain member of his class to his party because this boy 'always had a runny nose'.

Meeting up again for the first time after the school summer holidays, the mother of a girl I had entertained many times complained to me that lots of people had not come to her daughter's party during the holiday, a party Nina had not been invited to. I looked at her, thinking, *Are you for real?* But yes, indeed she *was* for real. I said, 'My mother died during the holiday,' to which she replied, 'Oh, I know how you feel. We had to have Jilly Rabbit put down,' and proceeded to give me chapter and verse on every traumatic vet visit. 'It was so awful!' she said, shaking her head, 'We had to leave her there for the vet to burn her.'

When Nina worried about not having any friends, I made the mistake of trying to reassure her that that was not the case, pointing out that plenty of children came to play at the house and to her parties. She replied, 'Of course they come to the house. It's a lovely house and we have great parties, but that doesn't mean that they are my friends or that they understand me.'

When she was fourteen, she wrote about this time: 'I had no idea there was something wrong with me; I just thought that popularity was something you were born with, and that I happened to have been born unpopular. I somehow thought that the fates had decreed that I would have no friends, which is a hard thing to take when you're ten.'

Twelve

The school gates were not my natural home, and as an introverted newcomer to the area, I felt isolated there. Many of the mothers were native to the town and indeed had attended the school themselves. '*She* was a right bitch!' I heard one remark as a PE teacher came into view. 'She used to bully me when I came to this school.'

One morning, I met this same young mother in Tesco beside the fruit and veg section. As we chatted, another woman pushed a trolley past laden with green and leafy fresh produce, and the young mother glanced sideways, rolled her eyes at the contents of the trolley, and said, 'Who does she think *she* is?'

It was hard to know how to fit in.

I got used to waiting on my own in the playground in anything from a thin, chill wind to an arctic blast, eventually investing in a huge black coat I could zip up beyond my chin and hide inside. If I could have zipped it right up to the top of my head, I probably would have. I was reminded of a mother that my sister Elizabeth had told me about years before, who waited at the school gates wearing a T-shirt with 'Another day, same old shit' written across it. I had been shocked at the time, but now felt a creeping admiration.

Looking back, I wonder if the other mothers noticed me and if they did, perhaps they thought *I* was the weird one. Perhaps I *was* the weird one. After all, I did once dress up six-year-old Lara as 'Roadkill' for the school Halloween disco – I got Cello to drive the Vauxhall Cavalier over a white T-shirt leaving tyre marks, I painted black crosses over her eyes and bought some bunny ears, which I bent into a downbeat angle. I thought it was hilarious and was amazed when she didn't win a prize.

Years later, as an adult, Lara showed photographs of this Roadkill outfit (now legendary in our family) to Spanish work colleagues in Madrid – who were reminiscing about costumes for carnival – and reported back that they were 'deeply shocked', so shocked in fact that the photo of her dressed as Roadkill made it into her work's newsletter.

It was always nerve-wracking waiting in the playground for Nina because who knew what damage another day at school might have wrought? What emotional state would she be in – exhausted, stressed, upset, hurt, angry – without being able to express why, because there were too many reasons why?

I would try to engage her in chat, but she didn't have head space for it after a day at school during which she had been masking her true self and working so hard to try to fit in. She would tell me, 'Stop cluttering up the room with words!'

It was very different waiting for Lara.

Nina and Lara came out at different times – of course they did – half an hour apart to create (it would seem) maximum inconvenience for the parents. Whenever I heard a politician (always a man) banging on about 'waging war on the school run', I felt like gnashing my teeth. Except my teeth were too busy chattering as I froze waiting at the school gates.

One day, I executed an impromptu tap dance in the school yard when I could see Lara's class lining up to leave. As the teacher's back was turned, I broke into Suzie Q, Suzie Q, step, ball, change, with extra jazz hands, and saw Lara's classmates popping their heads out of the line, one by one, mouths open. *Lara? Is that your Mum?*

'That was not easy for me,' remembered Lara many years later.

Yes, upon reflection, maybe it was me who was the weird one.

Twelve

Feelings of rejection took their toll on Nina, and she began to be overtaken by perfectionism. Maybe if she did everything perfectly, she would be accepted. If a piece of schoolwork wasn't up to her exacting standards, she would destroy it, ripping it up and putting it in the classroom bin. For Nina, if it wasn't exactly right, it was completely wrong.

When perfection becomes the only option, life becomes unbearable.

Homework was traumatising – seven-year-old Nina believed that schoolwork belonged at school and home was for other pursuits. I agreed with her, yet I went through the motions of trying to force her to conform and fit in. Pencils were snapped and thrown across the room, sheets were torn up (by Nina), voices raised (by both of us), and much misery created all for the sake of some silly worksheet that was too easy for her anyway.

And the irony was that I was taking her away from reading the books she loved to fulfil this pointless demand for homework. Left to her own devices, she would devour books on dinosaurs, planets and stars, rainforests, kings and queens, world religions, Greek myths – subjects she knew far more about that I ever would.

She was at her happiest when she was absorbed in a subject she was fascinated by. These subjects changed periodically. When her deep interest was outer space, I bought her a book full of images of stars and planets, and she delightedly took the scissors to it to make a scrap book. I stupidly got cross with her for defacing the book and insisted we stick the photograph back in the book. That book was never read again and remains, stuck back together, almost pristine, all present and correct, but unloved and unread on the shelves for evermore – indeed to this day – and I kick myself.

When she was immersed in a favourite subject, she would *live* it. I once took her to Tesco and said she could choose whatever she wanted for tea; she chose honey, bread, goats' cheese and grapes because, she said, that was what the Ancient Greeks would eat.

She loved *Harry Potter* and wrote to JK Rowling to ask who was the head of Hufflepuff House. Unlike the Queen and the Prime Minister, JK Rowling did not send back a personalised letter but a photocopied sheet pointing Nina in the direction of the fan club.

She also loved making collages, writing poems, cooking, dancing, trampolining, computer games and watching wildlife programmes. She was a seven-year-old Renaissance woman with a deep love of learning. She would read stories so fast that I doubted she had read them at all. 'How can you have finished it already?' I asked once, exasperated, just a few hours after I had given her a new novel. 'What happens in the end?' At which she recited the last page, and I opened the book and glanced down the final page in amazement.

Books meant a lot to Nina not just for the information they contained, but for the escape they provided. She was told off at school at least twice for reading. The first time was while eating her lunch where she was chided for not being sociable and chatting to the other children when, as Nina put it, 'no kid wanted to speak to me anyway'. And again, in class when she read too far ahead, which she was told was 'unfair on the other children'.

School was not made to fit Nina.

I walked into primary school one day at break to find Nina huddled under the coats in the cloakroom, biting her arms. Self-harming in this way was something Nina had done since

Twelve

nursery. She told me much later that she bit her arms as a kind of punishment when she had done something to annoy herself, or because she was angry and felt that no other option was open to her.

'Biting myself was better than biting someone else, and that was the only alternative besides "just stop feeling my feelings".'

All the other children were outside playing. Nina found the playground so overwhelming and unwelcoming that she had been hiding and no one had noticed – or at least no one had done anything about it. I didn't know how long this had been going on, but behind the water pipe beside her were lots of letters she should have brought home over the proceeding weeks. They weren't particularly important letters but for whatever reason, Nina had hidden them in this refuge under the coats.

Finding her alone and frightened and self-harming, I should have taken her home that day and never taken her back, but I had two children, and it was impossible to see how I could balance their needs if one was at school and the other not. I couldn't both jump off the world with Nina (as tempting as that was) and stay on it with Lara.

Shortly after I had found her hiding under the coats, and pointed this out to the school, the new headmistress banned parents from going inside the school building, except by appointment.

Another day, I got a call from the deputy head asking me to go to the school to rescue Nina who was apparently curled up in a ball on the playing field, refusing to go back into school. The teachers were afraid that if they approached her, she may bolt onto the road. I headed up there to discover her being shielded by Lara and her friends, who were trying to protect her. I walked up to them, smiling, and talking quietly, then held out my hand and Nina stood up and came with me. Seeing her there frightened and curled up like a terrified animal made me realise there had been no meaningful communication between me and the school at all.

So, in year three, Nina was recommended for assessment again. I would take her out of school one afternoon a week to an assessment centre where she was observed playing with other children at what they called the Dinosaur Group, or she would have art therapy. The aim of the group was to 'help children develop a better understanding of their feelings and to respond more appropriately to the emotional needs of others'.

Which now prompts me to ask: who was responding appropriately to Nina's emotional needs? Answer: no one.

I have discussed this assessment process with Nina as an adult and she says that despite being sent to better understand her feelings, she had never had the vaguest difficulty identifying what emotions she was experiencing at any given time. The problem had always been to get others to acknowledge and validate them.

Meanwhile, as Nina supposedly learned to better understand her feelings, I chatted with a psychologist, or joined a small parents' group, or sometimes I went to a nearby café and ate homemade soup, surrounded by people leading what I imagined to be normal lives, and I closed my eyes and breathed deeply, and *that* did me more good than anything else.

The psychologist at the assessment centre asked me about my childhood. I told her about my mother and her 'life is just one damned thing after another and it all goes from bad to worse' philosophy. For a moment, I wondered if it was Mark Twain who said that. But no, I think it was Margaret Simpson.

I was told I was over-compensating for the attention I did not get as a child by giving my child too much attention. I had

Twelve

to be more disciplined it seemed – I must set firm house rules and have suitable punishments to hand when the rules were infringed.

It was all my fault again, apparently – except now I was accused of giving her too much attention, rather than the *wrong sort* – and so the psychologists inducted me into the cult of the star chart and the naughty step.

There was a popular television programme in those days that advocated such child-rearing methods. These methods were apparently a parenting panacea and promised to work miracles with a regime of tough love, with their no-nonsense rules and rewards for good behaviour. This television programme was presumably enjoyed by the parents of cookie cutter children who fitted into this world, parents who could watch other parents (usually mothers) being shamed for having got it so *wrong*, tut, tut, tut.

At home, we went through the motions of having a family meeting to kick off this new regime and set up our house rules. We ended up with a sheet stuck to the fridge with a bland all-encompassing list of rules including: 'be kind', 'wait your turn', 'share your toys', 'listen carefully'. Star charts were headed up 'getting up with no fuss' and 'doing homework with no fuss', and stuck on the kitchen wall with promises of rewards for a full row of stars. What rewards? Freddo bars? Beanie Babies? I can't remember, but I know that the only reward Nina really wanted was not to have to go to school at all.

Twenty years later and fashions have changed. Parents are now warned against using rewards, which are considered short-term external motivators. Indeed, this style of parenting has been described by Gabor Maté, a specialist in childhood development and trauma, as 'obnoxious', but back in the noughties, it was all the rage.

The naughty step and the star charts did not make a blind bit of difference, of course. They were just something else for me to administer.

When Nina was upset, angry or uncooperative, forcing her to sit on the naughty step for five minutes where she would bite herself until her arm was studded with red indentations created more trouble than it solved, and no amount of Beanie Babies or Freddo bars could change the fact that Nina was trying to live on too few hours of sleep a night, constantly exhausted, and miserable and excluded at school.

At the weekends, she could enjoy deep refreshing sleep for as long as she wanted and wake up feeling good, but having to get up early all week for school was another way in which school was terrible for her health. Indeed, the circadian rhythms of people with autism and some other conditions usually naturally skew later.

It was at this time that she suggested to her art therapist at the Dinosaur Group that maybe she should take her purse out with her to hand out coins to reward people for being her best friend or letting her win at games. Perhaps the system of 'rewards' we had set up was making her believe that all interactions had to be transactional. She also got into trouble at school for giving chocolate to other children at lunch time. 'No sharing allowed,' she was told, and she was so upset to have got it wrong, again, despite trying to do something nice, that she flushed the rest of her Lindt 70 per cent down the toilet. 'It was such nice chocolate too,' commented the teacher with a tinkly laugh.

It was only years later that Nina and Lara told me, laughing, about how Cello's star chart parenting had gone rogue one evening when I was out at my tap dancing class. He had apparently offered them five pounds each to eat a plate of

Twelve

strawberries, which, unknown to him, they then threw at each other and hid under the sofa.

Despite this having happened a decade prior, he had the grace to look part amused but mainly shamed-faced at this recollection.

Thirteen

When I was a child, all rules were very much unwritten. There was no sign on the fridge, and there was certainly no psychologist to recommend one. However, rules were obeyed as if they were engraved on a tablet of stone brought down from Mount Sinai by my mother.

Rules like:

Thou shalt not ask questions that embarrass the family, such as *Why don't we see cousin Christine anymore? What did Uncle Ben do that was so bad? What's happened to Auntie Annie?* These questions were so taboo that I don't know the answers to this day.

Thou shalt not go in the spare bedroom and root in the interesting junk. Regardless that the stuff will lie abandoned for two generations and you will end up throwing it in a skip when you are fifty.

Thou shalt not turn off any news or current affairs programme, even if Dad is sound asleep, as he will immediately wake up and demand it back on.

Thou shalt not bring any animal into the house because they are filthy-dirty and only fit for the barnyard.

Thou shalt not break strict table manners; rules mainly to do with knives and elbows.

Plus, the great triumvirate of thou shalt nots: thou shalt not answer back, thou shalt not interrupt, and thou shalt not ignore me when I am talking to you. But far and away the most important from my mother, which encapsulated all the others, was THOU SHALT NOT SHOW ME UP. A commandment issued in caps.

The top and bottom was that adults were always right,

Thirteen

come what may, and to question that idea was disrespect of the highest order.

Cello tells me that when he was growing up, there were six rules spelled out by Giuseppe: do not get a tattoo, do not get your ear pierced, do not gamble, do not take drugs, do not smoke, and do not try homosexuality. Again, these were not on a sheet on the fridge but were verbalised loud and clear.

As grandparents, Giuseppe and Rosa's rules were all about keeping Nina and Lara safe. They ruled with fearful tales of a bear that lived in the fire if you got too close, a tiger in the oven, and a man on the street with a big black dog who would take you away if you were out without your parents.

Nina and Lara must have thought that life in a small flat on Easter Road was considerably more exciting than the actuality.

Rosa also added a dash of superstition: never burn bread because it's the body of Christ, and don't show off your good fortune or someone will afflict you with the evil eye, *Il Malocchio*. These superstitions were genuinely held; Cello remembered being five years old and his Aunt Filomena, in Southern Italy, heating olive oil to anoint him and 'drive out the demons' because some jealous person had made him ill by giving him the evil eye.

As Rosa aged and got weaker during the pandemic years, she began to believe someone had given her the evil eye over Facetime.

A generalised anxiety drove Rosa's parenting and grand-parenting, as well as specific fears. She lived in dread of the children choking on a rosemary stalk from the roast chicken, and when she cooked beef olives, there was barely suppressed hysteria at the potential for a cocktail stick-related injury. *Don't eat the stick! Mind the stick!*

Giuseppe loved giving advice and would stand at the door of his flat dispensing it as we clattered down the tenement steps. We would disappear from view with his shouted instructions echoing round the stone walls: 'Be good...Remember to start in first gear...Always drive on the left...'

My own father did not have specific rules but had more of a 'let's hope for the best' attitude to childcare, expressed by one of his favourite phrases: 'It'll be reet'.

He would take us on rides out – possibly to give my mother an hour's peace – to drop things off, pick things up, or pay farm bills at the ironmonger, the garage, the tractor repair shop or the vet.

Dad, it seemed, could talk forever to these people – where my mother was terse, my father was a talker, so long as the subject was farming. In retrospect, these conversations were strange things carried out in the Lancashire manner – much of the communication done by headshakes, 'Aye?!' and 'By 'eck's.

Sometimes it took a crisis to prise Dad away from his chatting – like six-year-old me in my best frock sitting in a wheelbarrow that had been freshly painted in green gloss, or on one memorable occasion, me wetting my pants and bursting into howling sobs. At which point Dad said, 'Ee, I'll be in trouble,' and then to me, 'It'll be reet,' and we headed home.

Once every six weeks, we'd go along for the ride as Dad took my grandad to the doctor's for his 'injections' (injections for what, we knew not, nor thought to ask). The outing to the doctor's included driving past a combine harvester parked in a Dutch barn – a highlight that necessitated Dad slowing down the car as we passed so we could admire the shiny, enormous redness of this exciting machine.

We also used to tag along to the knackers' yard where we were fascinated to see the knacker man sitting on a cow carcass eating his butties for dinner (the meal we ate at noon).

Thirteen

Strangely, I have a clearer memory of his dirty hands holding the white bread than what he was sitting on, which makes me wonder if maybe someone else told me about the knacker man sitting on the cow carcass and I've co-opted their memory.

One day, there was a trip out that was too boring even for us – and we were satisfied with very little. This time, Dad took us to the Inland Revenue in Preston where we sat in a windowless waiting room for what seemed like hours, eyes glued to the sliding hatch praying it would soon open and someone, *anyone*, would come out and help us.

But better than all these trips – and certainly better than the Inland Revenue – was going with Dad to the cattle auction at Lancaster or Preston. Preston was our favourite because it had the enormous stuffed head of a one-hundred-year-old shire horse called Honest Tom, which lived, dull-eyed, in a huge glass case and gazed out at us practically at our eye level.

We felt sorry for the terrified cows being led, shoved and pushed around the auction ring, and were fascinated by the auctioneer's gabble *WhatamIbid? WhatamIbid? I'mbid…I'mbid…two five, two five, two eight, two eight…* But even that novelty wore thin after a sale or two, and then we'd decide that racing round the top seats in the auditorium-like auction room was more fun, only realising after some minutes that the auctioneers' fast-talking had stopped and had turned into 'Would whoever is responsible for those children, please take charge of 'em!' And my father's head-shaking embarrassment: 'Yer little tykes.'

Dad may not have had strict rules for parenting, but he gave me some of the best advice I ever had: 'Write it down,' which he'd say whenever we discovered something interesting. 'Write it down in a little notebook.' My mother used to scoff at this advice, rolling her eyes, and as far as I know Dad never wrote it down himself. But I took his advice to heart.

I wrote diaries and lists of my favourite things. I made scrapbooks of my 'fav' pop stars and 'Fashions 1975' containing what I considered to be interesting trends of the day: 'Here are some beautiful platform boots…' and 'Here is the Queen in a rather old-fashioned hat…'

I wrote pen portraits of my relatives: 'Great Uncle Bill doesn't say much and just likes to wash up. His only story is how he once strangled a cat that got on the kitchen table…' 'Great Aunty Margaret wears a coat made of something called Astrakhan. She doesn't drink alcohol because she has signed the pledge, so people like to give her sherry trifle and laugh when she says "Ooh, that were good." She sings a song with the words "Tiddly-om-pom-pom…" in it.'

I interviewed family members: 'Tricia's fav group is Darts; she has an orange vinyl version of *Daddy Cool*…'

I wrote my own newspaper with the headline 'Stuart Simpson has started haymaking. Dennis Lawrenson has not.'

All grist to the mill for an eventual memoir writer.

Karl Ove Knausgård said that having a writer in the family is a curse. 'Write it down' was wonderful advice, but I'm not sure I am using it as Dad intended.

For all my rule following, my people pleasing, my not wanting to be a nuisance and fear of confrontation and my doing the right thing' delayed gratification, I think of the days when I broke the rules by skiving off high school, and instead hung out with my friends at the farm, as some of the happiest of my childhood.

By the time I was fifteen, my mother, who had an instinctive dislike of authority (unless it was her own), let me decide if it

Thirteen

was worth my time going to school or not – a form of benign neglect for which I was very grateful. If I decided I was unfit for PE lessons or too ill for school, that was up to me – and so was forging the necessary sicknote.

I remember summer days when my schoolmates hid out at the farm with me, being barefoot, eating sweets from the village Post Office, lying on the grass, a stick-to-my-teeth Opal Fruit melting in my mouth, eyes closed to the sun, and being happy.

I know now that breaking the rules may end up being the highlight of your life.

I look back on the way I raised my own children, now they are young women, and I ask myself something much more important, it turns out, than how to teach them to follow the rules: I ask myself, in what ways did I teach them to disobey?

As an adult, Nina rues the fact that she was over-protected as a child and not treated with a bit more benign neglect, and says, 'To be over-protected is to miss a million tiny opportunities.'

Fourteen

After Nina's attendance at the Dinosaur Group, when she was aged seven, I was told that she had 'no hard wiring problem such as ADHD or autism', and it was up to me to get the parenting right. They noted that her 'strong-willed temperament made her a difficult child to rear'.

I was given tuition in how to play with her, which seemed like being taken right back to the drawing board, parenting 101. I had apparently been doing this most fundamental thing – you would assume *instinctive* thing – wrong.

I was instructed that instead of asking questions about the picture she was creating, which could be intrusive and make her defensive, or praising her for her 'beautiful' drawing, I must make statements – a sort of running commentary – on her play: *You've picked up a red crayon, you've drawn a box, you've coloured it in blue.*

It seemed counterintuitive not to praise her, and rather forced and artificial to act like a compere, but this approach did seem to make Nina more relaxed.

I was devastated that I had been making a mess of it, but I lived in hope that some piece of advice would be a turning point for us. The report from this second assessment noted that I 'participated eagerly and profitably' with them – 'eagerly' I think because I was desperate for help of any kind, and 'profitably' presumably because my smiling mask and optimism made them think we were making more headway than we actually were.

I was also told I had set unattainably high standards in the behaviour I was expecting from Nina and was recommended a book called *The Good Enough Child: How to Have an Imperfect*

Fourteen

Family and be Perfectly Satisfied.

So, it seemed having been told in the past that I was expecting too little of her, and more discipline was required, I was now being told I was expecting too much.

Nina obviously discovered this *Good Enough Child* book some time later; she never mentioned it, but I found it partially ripped up and shoved behind the bookcase, as though the world's strongest man had tried to tear through a telephone directory.

Outside school, I ferried Nina on an endless round of clubs: trampoline, Rainbows, Brownies, swimming, horse riding, karate, football, street dance, ballet, digital music; a search for something she would enjoy and somewhere she would feel at home.

'Oh, you've created your own social therapy,' commented the doctor.

I soon got to know which group leaders could communicate with Nina and which could not. 'What is wrong with her?' bellowed the renowned karate teacher, who was clearly more renowned for karate than for teaching, and who burst out of the gym hall to remonstrate with me as Nina ran round and round his class in a panic while the remaining pupils watched silently, lined up at the side.

I would sit outside all these classes, trying to look relaxed with a book or a magazine, knowing that at any moment I may be called on to intervene, that I may have to whisk Nina away from people who did not get her.

However, despite the ranting, unhelpful coach, I remained apologetic. I had a don't rock the boat attitude, a don't confront, don't ask for anything, keep smiling attitude in case any other attitude made Nina even more vulnerable than she already was.

Hold Fast

Keeping the world on side felt like a huge responsibility.

Sometimes I would attend classes alongside her, so after school on a Wednesday, Nina joined an art class full of pensioners and me, where, while I painstakingly picked out little flowers and painted pictures of tea cups in watercolours, she created remarkable still lives of vases of vibrant flowers and psychedelic fruit bowls in acrylic primary colours – working 'with gay abandon', as the teacher remarked – many of which still hang on my walls twenty years later.

There was a panic imbued in many of these extra-curricular activities: I must book them! All the child-rearing books say so! Nina must go! Everyone else goes! We must be normal!

Why? Why normal? What was my obsession with following all the rules?

It was probably because I felt there was one small window of opportunity to introduce Nina to the world and help her adjust to it, and that window was NOW.

I had swallowed hook, line and sinker the idea that all these extra-curricular activities would help Nina fit in with her peers; that they would help her enjoy mixing and taking part in teamwork and that she would then magically be able to communicate better and would work well with others. She would make new friends! The parenting books were so certain about this – no doubts expressed that some children may be different.

So, I persisted with the delusion that this packed itinerary of extra-curricular activities was a solution, even when the evidence of my own eyes told me it was often a problem.

There was nothing relaxed about this dash from activity to activity, and if Nina (and later, Lara) expressed reluctance to go to these classes – which were supposed to be fun and done in their spare time – I was conflicted between persuading them to stick it out (especially if new shoes, clothing or equipment

Fourteen

had already been bought), or not taking them and therefore wasting the money and feeling like a failure.

What these classes also provided, in theory, besides all the magical effects listed above, was forty-five minutes of peace for me to relax (or more likely bite my nails, or stare into space) as I waited outside. Unallocated time felt like a gift, but, as with the case of the irate karate teacher, the reality was often different, and rather than providing me with a short oasis of peace, going to the classes only increased pressure on us all – especially when things went spectacularly wrong – and extracted a toll out of proportion to any benefit. When a class was unexpectedly cancelled, I considered it being let off the hook.

But I persisted, getting increasingly exhausted, feeling heavy and sluggish, and fantasising about sleep and resting my head on a pillow.

'Stop trying to run the world,' it says in my diary from that time. 'Stop trying so hard.' It continues: 'I am writing this faster and faster because I feel guilty just sitting here. Hurry. Hurry. Hurry.'

I remember one evening waiting in the car outside Nina's Rainbows meeting, where she was no doubt making autumn decorations or learning a new song. It was September 11th 2001; the radio played as I gripped the steering wheel, watching the dusk set in, listening to the unbelievable news reports from New York about the Twin Towers. I found myself holding my breath, and for once imagining what was happening behind the closed doors of the Rainbows meeting was less stressful than hearing what was happening in the outside world.

My diary at the time contained a list of advice I wrote to myself:

- Prioritise sleep.
- Take action. (Sometimes that action might be just to have a cup of tea.)
- You're an adult – you don't need permission.
- You can go your own way – you don't always have to fit in.
- Speak up.
- Don't drift – decide.
- Enjoy the here and now.
- If it's not your responsibility don't accept it.
- Don't be so conscientious about things that don't matter.
- To be a good mother, you must look after yourself first.

I knew the theory. I just couldn't live it.

Another reason for having a packed schedule was because Nina always asked me first thing in the morning, 'What are we doing today?' And several times during the day, 'What are we doing next?' I felt the pressure to have an answer – it took me years to realise that she was asking because she hated surprises and wanted to know her schedule, not because she was pressuring me to arrange yet another activity.

By contrast with Nina and Lara's organised childhood, I had spent my childhood evenings and weekends running around the fields, woods, barns and farmyard with my sisters, playing catch, making dens and searching for kittens, or indoors watching hours of television, drawing, dressing up, or reading *Five Go to Smuggler's Top* for the umpteenth time: activities largely independent of adults. At the beginning of the summer holidays, when my mother gave each of us a set of ten felt pens and a new drawing book, she left us to decide what to put in it, and we were thrilled at the promise of those seemingly endless, empty pages and the freedom they offered.

Fourteen

Our lives as children were regulated by the church calendar and the farming seasons: harvest festival, Advent, Christmas, Easter, Mothering Sunday, silaging, hay making; all requiring different hymns or different songs, different outfits, different homemade cards and gifts.

Our children were not tethered in this way – not to the farm and not to the church.

When Cello and I got married, a Catholic priest had officiated alongside our Church of England vicar in the church where I had been confirmed and beside the churchyard where several generations of my family lay buried. Both children were later christened into the Catholic church, but it was really a gesture for old times' sake because our faith was hanging by a thread, if not broken, by then. For a time, we took the children to church on a Sunday just so they would know the rituals, the words, the mysteries of that world should they ever need or want it.

Nina walked out of her first confession lesson saying she didn't want to be a Catholic anyway, she wanted to be a Protestant because it was easier. She made her first confession – confessing to hitting her little sister – to a skin-head priest whose Doc Martens were visible under his cassock as he lounged on the pew to listen. He was a renegade priest who was famous for attending a séance and saying, "Oh, ghost, do fuck off". He was eventually driven out of the diocese for remarrying divorcees and blessing gay relationships, but for a time he had them (and us) packing out the pews and sitting in the aisles every Sunday.

But when Steve the Priest left, we left too. 'Why did we like him so much?' I ask Cello now, to which he replies, 'Well, er, well...He wasn't a cunt.'

My sisters and I were taken to Sunday school in the village church every week and some of our carvings are still, shamefully, visible on the back seat pews to this day. Uncle Dennis and Aunty Dorothy took us along, and although it was ostensibly our choice whether to go or not, I suspect my mother urged us to polish our shoes and get ready because it got us out from under her feet for an hour or two.

Sunday school amounted to the vicar telling us the same story every week of how his church was bombed in Coventry during the Second World War and his Jesus statue was blown to smithereens, only to be painstakingly reassembled – 'See, here it is!' – while we wriggled on the itchy carpeted seats and felt jealous of the little ones drawing Noah's ark in the vestry with Aunty Dorothy.

My mother took me and my older sister, Elizabeth, to weekly piano lessons for a few years because she wanted us to be as musical as she was, but she was perpetually disappointed and ended up resorting to paying us to do our piano practice instead of receiving any pocket money (two and a half pence per fifteen minutes, if I remember correctly) – which did nothing to improve our piano playing and only succeeded in enraging my Victorian grandad. *You get paid to practise yon pian-er!*

Years later, I stumbled upon the phrase 'benign neglect', and it rang bells: we were left to our own devices a lot. It is sometimes suggested that benign neglect in parenting can benefit children in a way that continual attention does not. It is said that benign neglect encourages children to explore, make choices and problem solve, and that it gives them a sense of autonomy.

Maybe I was too young for it, or maybe the balance between benign neglect and attention was skewed, but a strong memory I have of growing up on the farm is one of boredom – or at least that was how I then described the feeling to myself,

Fourteen

although as an adult I may identify it is as sadness, loneliness or depression. Mum always said, 'Only boring people get bored, Catherine!' so I rarely used the word out loud, but it was a feeling that often settled upon me when the farm was quiet – when Dad was working down the fields and Mum was shut in her bedroom 'tired', when there was nothing but the testcard on the television and the world seemed stagnant and lonely and sad.

I would stare out of the living room window at the pig crew and the giant oak tree opposite, a tree that had cast its shadow over the farm gate as long as anyone could remember. As an adult, I know that that tree must have been a haven for hundreds of insects and animals, but on those dead days it seemed to me that not a creature was stirring, not even a mouse. At times like these, the farm seemed like a claustrophobic trap, an isolated, oppressive place where the air was heavy, where I felt alone and numb, and the world was meaningless, hopeless and empty of everything bar swirling dust motes, and even those appeared to have slowed down. Time was interminable and I longed to escape to anywhere, absolutely anywhere but there.

One day, relief came in the form of an episode of *Play Away* on BBC2 where a kind-faced man called Brian Cant sang and danced and generally exuded happiness. Brian Cant looked like a man who was glad to be alive, a man who could find joy in anything, anywhere. I was enthralled by him. What a blessing, what a tonic, what an impossibility he was. I remember clutching the windowsill, my attention diverted from the static oak and the dust motes trapped in a shaft of light, and I thought maybe one day I would marry a jolly, kind-faced man like Brian Cant, a man who sang and danced and laughed and acted the fool just for the fun of it, and on that day I would look back on this empty day and I would remember it.

Hold Fast

I did marry a kind man – although he bore little resemblance to Brian Cant, and in fact was more likely to bring to mind PG Wodehouse's quote about it 'never being difficult tell the difference between a ray of sunshine and a Scotsman with a grudge' – but on my wedding day at the farm, when 120 guests passed under the old oak tree and milled about between the marquee and the farmhouse, I did not look back on that empty day because just briefly, I had forgotten it.

Looking back at those sad, empty days, it appears more like a case of childhood depression (something I now understand that I definitely had from at least the age of twelve) but when I was younger than that – seven or eight – I called it 'boredom', and by the time I had my own children I was still thinking back to it as that.

In the seventies, of course, no one of our class – the farming class – had depression even as adults. Instead, they had 'bad nerves' or 'an unstable mind', and for a child to be so afflicted would have been unthinkable.

I couldn't bear my children to say they were bored because I did not want them to feel as empty and lonely as I had felt as a child, so a subconscious desire to chase away familiar feelings of sadness and hopelessness was another factor fuelling the mad ricochet between extra-curricular activities.

Some argue that boredom is good for children as it encourages the brain to seek stimulation, to escape the unpleasant sensation of boredom, and therefore it encourages creativity. This may be true: I do remember the glorious sensation of hitting upon a new project as a child – of 'cleaning up' the woodland (with a dustpan and brush), of building a new house for my Tressy doll, or of starting to write a new book or a play ('The Adventures of...') – but much stronger than those memories are the crushing memories of what I

Fourteen

thought of as boredom, that dead, stale, joyless feeling of utter meaninglessness.

Perhaps it is no coincidence that the leisure activities my children have chosen as adults are entirely different from the classes I dragooned them to as children. Nowadays there is no ballet, horse riding, karate or football for girls, but instead they enjoy speaking German and Spanish, hiking, kayaking, baking, blues dancing, techno music, Japanese food, wild camping, cold water swimming and gaming, all passions they have discovered without my help.

The obsession with being 'normal' was in fact a desire for my child to be accepted by the world.

Who really wants to be normal (definition: usual, typical, expected, conforming, commonplace, indistinct)? Surely we would all prefer to be extraordinary, special or outstanding? Lots of things are normal, but that does not make them desirable. For some people, shouting at their children is normal, eating too much junk food is normal, watching too much television is normal, but they are not desirable.

The lure of normal becomes strong when you have a vulnerable child who experiences rejection in the outside world.

For a parent faced with that sort of pain, a state of normality becomes highly desirable to protect them. You want them to blend into the crowd. You secretly believe them to be extraordinary, but you want them to demonstrate their extraordinariness in modest and acceptable ways – passing Grade 1 piano, perhaps, or being able to recite *The Owl and the Pussycat* from start to finish. Extraordinary in these small ways may be fine, but being abnormal is not at all fine, for fear of attracting the wrong kind of attention.

Hold Fast

There is much talk of difference being respected, but talk is often all it is, and school is a particularly dangerous environment in which to stand out. In fact, you stand out at your peril. There is a tyranny of normality and children are adept at spotting those who fall outside these parameters. There is safety in numbers, so understandably everyone wants to belong to the group and to do so – to be accepted, to be acceptable – you must be considered normal. You must be the same as everyone else. When Nina was at school, there were strict restrictions on what was the acceptable way to be a boy and what was the acceptable way to be a girl, and woe betide you if you fell outside these restrictions.

It is a challenge for any parent to balance the urge to expose their child to the world while simultaneously shielding them from it – and with a child who is in some way different, this balance is all the more precarious. The consequences of too much exposing can be catastrophic for their self-esteem, yet too much shielding leaves them dangerously vulnerable when you are not there.

I became very aware of the other children in her class who I could now identify as also being in some way different; children who would probably have gone under my radar if I was not going through the experience of mothering Nina. Children who were obviously neglected, children who were very fat or very thin, children who radiated enormous vulnerability, possibly neurodivergence, and often loneliness. Hence the strict instructions about inviting either fewer than half the class or all the class to any party we had.

Back then it was the unknown unknowns that often caused the most trouble for us. What financiers call black swan events – a

Fourteen

negative occurrence that is impossible to predict, unexpected and unknowable. We knew about Nina's phobia of nettles – a phobia that could send her running into traffic to avoid them and that soon extended to include bees, wasps and jellyfish – and we knew about the terrible fear of drains that would send her hysterical in a swimming class. We knew about the hatred of people with dirty ears (usually little boys), which could cause all sorts of embarrassment in social settings.

We could try to find solutions to deal with these situations and negotiate our way through each day, but always there were new fears and phobias, tomorrow's unknown problems that could easily become today's surprise challenges – the unknown unknowns, the traps just waiting to be sprung.

One day, six-year-old Nina started to worry about her car and home insurance when she was an adult. She had seen the zooming red telephone Direct Line adverts on the television and was inconsolable. 'How will I know which to choose? It says it's a "good deal better". But *how will I know?*'

She explained to me years later that the reason she was so concerned about adult things like car insurance was because she thought dealing with adult life was the reason she had to go to school, and she reasoned that adult life must be incredibly important to get right if she had to endure something as terrible as school for its sake.

It was a delicate balancing act between reassuring her too much (in which case, the experts warned me, the fear became more grounded and could become obsessive) or not reassuring her enough (in which case, the fear grew rampant and unchecked).

We truly never knew where or when the next unknown would burst forth. Nina's panic was never far from the surface. Day-to-day problems were not always anxiety-related

– sometimes, they were due to her senses being much more sensitive than ours.

She felt hunger pangs very strongly and as soon as she did, she would fear starvation. 'Friends and family are mere trifles in comparison to pizza,' she said, in all seriousness, as she dashed towards a pizzeria in Southern Italy without waiting for the rest of our party. The upside of this ability to taste intensely was that she got *enormous* pleasure from food. One of Nina's first proper meals as a baby had been a bowl of Italian soup - *capellini,* thin spaghetti in a chicken broth beaten through with egg. Upon tasting it from a plastic spoon wielded by me, she'd grabbed the bowl with both hands and tried to down it in one. *Real food, at last!* she seemed to be saying. *Give me this, and no more of that baby rice mouléd pap!*

If she was warm in the car, she would fear getting boiling hot followed by dehydration and death – *Turn the sun off! Turn it off!*

Catastrophising was her default setting.

She was obviously highly intelligent and articulate, and yet we struggled to use words to address her fears.

We constantly operated in a stressful environment which, if the intensity could have been measurable on the Beaufort wind force scale, would have varied from a rare number 2 light breeze, through an everyday number 6 strong breeze, to a relatively common number 10 storm, but often out of the blue, number 12 hurricane force.

I spent a lot of time in crisis mode – constantly vigilant for potential disaster, waiting for the next hurricane force, a state of watchfulness that made life intense and exhausting.

As a little girl, I was always hoping for good luck and I would count out sweets in a jar, pencils in a case, petals on a daisy trying to foresee it: lucky, unlucky, lucky, unlucky. Would everything work out all right? I would pull the petals off one

Fourteen

by one: lucky, unlucky, lucky, unlucky, as I searched for reassurance. Would everything be ok? Would my wishes come true?

Now I had become the kind of woman who kept lucky crystals in her pocket – blue agate, cold, smooth and soothing in my palm. I was the kind of woman who wore silver sixpence lucky charms around her neck and had good luck symbols dangling from her handbag; I was festooned in talismans, hoping they had the power to protect. I was the kind of woman who repeated mantras like 'Everything is working out perfectly' in an increasingly desperate inner voice, or who sometimes used the words of Julian of Norwich: 'All shall be well, and all shall be well and all manner of thing shall be well,' a phrase that makes Julian of Norwich sound as desperate for reassurance as me.

From moment to moment, life was precarious, and it often felt like only magic could help.

Nina devised her own coping strategies, some more helpful than others. Having seen programmes on television where wild cats protected themselves by growling, she began to bare her teeth and growl when she was upset.

Another of her coping mechanisms was for her to write a letter to the manager, on hotel stationery, as soon as we arrived on holiday:

My complaints to the manager
1. There is no kettle here.
2. You make us wear rubbish bath hats in the pool.
3. The shampoo stinks.
4. The window in the bathroom is not frosted.

All reasonable points, to be fair. We had many enjoyable foreign holidays, despite someone remarking, pointedly, 'People with a child *like yours* might consider buying a motorhome.'

We didn't.

Hold Fast

Sometimes the real world intruded and caused Nina quite reasonable worries. The day after her eighth birthday, the Second Gulf War broke out and Nina wrote her own newspaper: *Tony Blair has still to decide about a possible third world war. HELP! By tomorrow, there could be bombs landing all over Edinburgh!!! The decisions are being made tonight. Please keep your fingers crossed everyone, because no one (well not much people) want a third world war.*

To stop myself constantly focussing on what was difficult about motherhood, I started a praise journal in which I listed a whole page of things the girls had done well each day, and we wrote it together:

Lara carefully looked after the woodlouse in her woodlouse house…Nina shared her alien with Lara…Lara was honest when asked who had coloured in the keyboard…Nina played Baboons very cooperatively and let Emily be Main Baboon with good humour…

Then they would reciprocate by doing a page for me – 'Mummy *smiled at her children…Mummy gave her children a hug…Mummy let her children spend their birthday money on Beanie Babies…*' – and Cello: '*Daddy worked hard…Daddy used nice language and stayed good humoured even when Rangers scored…*'

When we were children, Mum had told us to be quiet in many different ways: 'Speak when you're spoken to, stop being so giddy, stop interrupting, little pigs have big ears, stop mithering, stop yer moidering, hush!' But conversely if you said nothing, or tried to say it quickly to get it over with and stop being a nuisance, the response was 'Has the cat got your tongue?' or 'Stop muttering, don't mumble, speak slower!', or the most unnerving: 'Enunciate!'

Fourteen

I had vowed that I would talk to my children and encourage them to have opinions, to ask questions and to join in. I longed to know what my children thought.

Of course, my bluff was called by Nina who thought nothing of saying exactly what she thought (while she was with us at home, at least). She considered this not to be rude but honest – and hadn't we always told her to be honest? 'Ugly family alert,' she said as some guests she didn't know walked up our garden path, and my heart stopped, only for her to get a closer look and announce, 'Alert called off.'

My mother continued to try to put us on mute throughout our teenage years. When I was fifteen, Kate Bush burst into my life and onto the world stage, and more to the point on to Thursday night's *Top of the Pops* – sensual, sexy, mixing literature with music with dancing, art and philosophy. She was and still is a hero of mine. My school friend, Carole, gleefully remembers phoning me one evening and my mother answering the phone and calling upstairs, 'Catherine! Phone! And will you *turn down* that wailing woman!'

Fifteen

When Nina was five and Lara two, I had started doing freelance journalism.

Cello was freelance by then too, so I could work alongside him. In truth, we could not both be out of the house at the same time because one of us had to be available to down tools and head to nursery or school if there was an emergency.

One such emergency was a phone call from the nursery with the alarming news that Nina was unable to shut her mouth and was drooling and bleeding, and could we go immediately? We dashed there, throwing our coats on as we ran to the car, wondering, *what fresh hell is this?*

At the nursery, Cello peered into Nina's mouth and recoiled, as the staff hovered, holding their breaths. I took a look and asked, 'Er, what did you have at snack time…?' as I watched the strawberry jam from a Jammy Dodger that was wedged in her palate drip down her chin.

So not all emergencies were true emergencies, however enough of them *were* real emergencies to make going out to work feel like freedom.

I enjoyed interviewing people with stories to tell for *Woman's Own, Woman* and other magazines. It was like jumping off the planet for a time, visiting people in their homes up and down the country listening to tales of illness, miraculous recovery, dramatic weight loss, plastic surgery, violence, crime, love against the odds, weddings from hell, holidays from hell, friends from hell, anything from hell, love triangles and love rats, oh so many love rats, for which the magazines had an insatiable appetite.

Fifteen

Writing these stories gave me a break from my own story. Other people's worries took my mind off my own worries as I tried to make sense of 'my boyfriend left me for my stepmother and now I babysit their twins', or 'my son's friend was a vampire who killed him and drank his blood', and other convoluted human dramas and unimaginable tragedies. People often asked if we made these stories up – indeed, they assumed that we did – but I learned while writing for magazines that real life was far more outlandish than fiction. I found I had a talent for meeting and talking to people, for immersing myself into other people's worlds and writing a good story.

The difficulty came when I had to deal with the commissioning editors at the magazines. Since leaving office-based work, I had lost all confidence in being part of the world of work. My heart raced and I felt sick if I had to pick up the phone and speak to the magazine's head office. 'Hello, Hun…' they would sing-song at me, insincerely. 'How are you, sweetie?' I could interview and write features until the cows came home but I couldn't pretend to be comfortable with these over-familiar, southern office dwellers; people I had never set eyes on but who addressed me like a long-lost friend.

I had to psych myself up before I lifted the receiver – literally sweating and deep breathing as I glanced around my makeshift office in the attic, surrounded by the flotsam and jetsam of our lives: dusty stacks of files marked 'buying house' or 'receipts for new bathroom', next to a big trunk of Christmas decorations oozing tinsel, piles of outgrown baby suits and tiny dresses, and the boxes of scrap material I planned to use to make patchwork quilts and rag rugs, plus an old cardboard suitcase brought to Scotland by Cello's father when he emigrated here and which now contained the sugar icing flowers from our wedding cake and two bundles of new baby cards. All this life detritus piling up around me, a world away from the clean, shiny, efficient office world I imagined I was phoning.

I would probably have felt better if I could have stood up, but the office was an illegal one, knocked together by our friendly joiner from Formica kitchen surfaces and squeezed into a too-small space below the low sloping attic roof. Sitting there, you were left feeling like the weight of the world was resting on your shoulders, and it meant there was only room to sit and spin, not stand.

All I needed to know from the sing-song people at head office was 'How many words do you want?' and 'When is the deadline?', but these interactions seemed like an insurmountable ordeal – a call to occupants of another planet.

Cello suggested I see a therapist.

This time, the therapist was glamorous, kind and full of life, and I trusted her immediately. She looked like someone who had got her own life in order and therefore, I thought, maybe she could help me do the same. I explained my panic at picking up the phone to these London-based magazines – maybe I had a phobia about telephones, I suggested.

She listened sympathetically, then explained the term 'imposter syndrome'. I had lost so much confidence since leaving work that, despite my communications degree and journalism training, I apparently saw myself as a fraud and was terrified of being found out. I apparently could not believe that I deserved any success workwise.

When she spelled it out to me, it seemed ridiculous.

She gave me breathing and visualisation techniques to help me phone the editorial teams in London without wanting to throw up, but having had my fears exposed to the light of day, they had shrivelled away. 'I can tell within twenty minutes if therapy will work,' she said, and it seemed she was right with me.

Fifteen

Small acts of kindness towards Nina made a huge impression on me. When Nina was inconsolable during her first flight – 'Nuff sky! Nuff sky!' – a Japanese traveller made her an origami crane, which was handed back from seat to seat, passenger to passenger, to distract her. The night before her first day at school, a neighbour brought round a *Schultüte* – a cone of presents to wish her well.

Her Uncle Rino, Cello's brother, who had not picked up a felt pen since primary school, would hunch down beside her little table and draw the Teletubbies over and over again, singing the theme tune: 'Tinky-Winky, Dipsy, Laa-Laa, Po'. He spent hours recreating her favourite *Teletubbies* episode, carrying her high over his head at an excruciating arms' length – *Flying like Po!* – while Nina held her toy Po at arm's length. *Flying like Po!* He took her to the butterfly farm despite hating creepy crawlies.

All these acts of kindness were appreciated hugely, especially now we knew how unkind and unwelcoming the world could be.

One of the most surprising things Nina did to fit in was joining the cheerleading team. I took her along each week to the leisure centre where she leapt about and shook pom poms and clapped and jumped. It all seemed harmless, until the teacher mentioned 'the Nationals'. My heart sank. Did even cheerleading have to be competitive? Nina hated competitive team sports because other members got angry with her if they thought she had done something wrong. 'Why didn't you pass it?!' a ten-year-old girl had screamed in Nina's face at her first football for girls class. Combined with her perfectionism, this sort of interaction was agonising for her.

'Oh, it's not competitive,' the cheerleading coach assured

me. 'It's not really a competition at all.' She dazzled me with her great big smile: 'It's all good fun. She'll love it. I promise!'

This was one of those moments when I had to decide: do I go for it and encourage Nina to have a new experience, or do I nip this in the bud right away and refuse to have anything to do with it for all our sakes? Do I expose her or shield her? As usual, because I feared not putting in enough effort, I went for the 'encourage Nina to have a new experience' exposure option.

On the day of the Nationals, we piled into a bus for the seventy-mile trip to Dundee. On arrival, we found the Caird Hall with its Doric columns flapping with banners to welcome cheerleaders from all over the country, as the name the Nationals implied. As for it 'not being a competition', the air bristled with adrenaline, high excitement, hairspray and competitiveness before we'd even got off the bus.

In the packed auditorium, which had previously hosted the biggest names in show business including The Beatles, Frank Sinatra and Bob Hope, mothers chanted and sang. It had the feel of a Roman amphitheatre and I dreaded to think who was being thrown to the lions today. The over-excited supporters were blowing whistles and horns, waving banners and placards, and wearing T-shirts with 'Team Mom' on the back.

This was another world, and my sense of foreboding was deep.

After going with Nina to the changing room and making sure she was lycraed-up and with her high ponytail sprayed and pinned in place, I took a seat in the auditorium. I put Kate Bush on my iPod, held my earphones tight to my ears, closed my eyes and tried to have an out-of-body experience – anywhere but here, anywhere but here in the Caird Hall with a million hyper cheerleaders and their over-invested 'moms'.

Fifteen

I could barely breathe as Nina's group danced – as if by sheer strength of will and the power of my mind, I could make everything all right. I couldn't. They came bottom in the first round, and the second, and every subsequent round after that. Unfortunately, after each round, the results were announced very loudly and very publicly: 'And in seventh place out of seven, we have…' 'And in fifth place out of five, we have…' The team's disappointment was palpable, obvious in their sagging body language, even across the vast expanse of the hall. In my place at the back of the auditorium, I felt my throat constrict, my stomach tie in knots, my breathing turn shallow.

I nipped outside for some fresh air and, this being Dundee and the home of *The Dandy* and *The Beano*, I stood beside the statue of Minnie the Minx with her mischievous expression and her sling shot, a character who never felt the need to conform or to fit in. At least *she* was having fun. Back inside, I couldn't find Nina in the changing room, and eventually spotted her wandering the corridors on her own looking agitated. She didn't like it, she said. She didn't like stupid cheerleading anymore. She wanted to go home, she wanted to go home *now*.

Another lesson I should have learned by then: never get trapped anywhere with Nina where you are dependent on others to be able to leave and where you can't make an immediate exit.

At lunch time, I took Nina to a nearby restaurant, and we treated ourselves to a tasty grown-up meal and I had a glass of wine and pretended I was somewhere sensible and not at the Cheerleading Nationals. I didn't find out what the other mothers were doing for lunch – I too had run out of fitting-in energy. I couldn't escape this adventure quickly enough, but seeing as we were stuck there for the day, we may as well make the most of it by having a civilised meal. In fact, it was a balm, being just the two of us in our own world for an hour.

Hold Fast

Back to the Caird Hall for the afternoon, and the event limped to a close without the team having won a single point. As we headed for the bus home (me now with a spring in my step), I caught sight of the previously perky cheerleading coach, the lady with the great big smile and promises of 'it's all good fun'. She was now openly weeping, tears streaming down her face, her eyeliner in streaks across her cheeks. The assistant coach was gripping her by the shoulders as they staggered, bereft, towards the bus.

Sixteen

My mother had talked about going on a cruise for years but there was always the farm to keep them at home – silaging, hay making, cows calving, twice-daily milkings – but for their twentieth wedding anniversary, she booked the two of them on a cruise on the *QE2* to New York. Five days away from the farm (and us). We were teenagers and would be left on the farm with our grandad.

Dad was measured up for a blazer, Mum ran up some 'formal, captain's dinner' and some 'smart but casual' attire on her sewing machine – it was action stations. This *QE2* experience would surely become one of those landmark events in our family history. An event that would go down in legend, like when Grandma and Grandad went to stay at Treetops Hotel in Kenya where Princess Elizabeth found out she had become Queen.

Then one morning, I got up to find Mum standing in a simmering rage at the stove, speechless with fury. 'What's the matter?' I asked, but answer came there none, just a wordless outrage. I saw a letter balanced on the milk jug in the middle of the kitchen table and picked it up to read. It informed my mother that the *QE2* would have to go into dry dock for repairs on the dates she had booked. They were very sorry, full of apologies and all that, but the cruise was cancelled.

The horror! The horror!

Would she like to book another date? enquired the letter, but of course with the demands of a busy dairy farm those dates had been the one chance for her and Dad to go on a cruise. They were the only suitable dates, *and my mother had been denied.*

I can still feel the gut-wrenching guilt, the *oh my God, will we ever get over this?* The sense of helpless, stomach-churning anxiety that due to this cruel twist, my mother would be crushed by disappointment, and that we – the rest of the family – were in some way responsible. Of course, there was nothing I could do and nothing consoling I could say. 'Oh, heck,' I muttered, pathetically, before replacing the letter on the milk jug and sidling out of the way. The cruise never happened, the blazer never got worn, the captain's table was never graced, the smart but casual had to wait for another day.

My mother had a habit of harbouring dreams that did not come true. She had chosen not to have an engagement ring ('What's *engaged?* You're either married or you're not!') but she always told us that she dreamed of having an emerald eternity ring. 'Emeralds are more precious than diamonds,' she would tell us. 'They are *rarer*.' But her emerald eternity ring never materialised, presumably because she never suggested to Dad that they actually go and buy it – something my dad would have been happy to do but would never have taken the initiative to organise. It can't have been lack of money because the eighties were years of plenty for farmers; indeed, for her silver wedding, Mum got a mink coat with her name embroidered on the satin lining – a coat she appeared to be delighted with but that I rarely saw her wear.

Likewise, it seemed that after the *QE2* nonstarter, cruising would become another mythical pleasure my mother had been denied by the fates. So, twenty years later, when my mother had still never been on a cruise and had by this time already been treated for cancer, I decided that Cello and I would book a cruise for us and our children, and we would take Mum and Dad along. Otherwise, it would be too late – and, like the emerald eternity ring, it would fail to happen, and somebody somewhere might hold me responsible.

Sixteen

On the cruise with Mum and Dad, Dad always wanted to see all there was to see whilst Mum would not sit in the bar or watch the entertainment unless Cello and I went with them. There was no child care for our primary school-aged children, so I would feel obliged to keep the children up past their bedtimes – when all Cello and I wanted to do was crash out exhausted in our cabin – so we could encourage Mum to agree to go out and 'enjoy' herself, which would then enable Dad to go out and soak up the atmosphere.

Impossibly, we were trying to make everyone happy. As I drank over-priced wine in the ship's lounge, accompanied by over-tired children, to the backdrop of a Beatles tribute band or a tinkling piano, I noted that no good deed ever goes unpunished.

On the cruise, we visited the Captain's Bridge to see where the Greek captain and his crew managed the ship's navigation. There was a bank of flashing screens including radar and other up-to-date electronic navigation systems. Next to them was a huge table covered in nautical maps and sea charts, compasses, barometers and a sextant for celestial navigation, and on a ledge above was a row of plaster saints and gold-edged holy cards, including depictions of St Nicholas, the patron saint of seafarers, all festooned in prayer beads. This Greek captain with his belt-and-braces approach to safety and getting us all there in one piece reminded me of my approach to navigating my way through parenting Nina – get help from the best most up-to-date experts, use the supposed tried and tested methods, and when all else fails, keep the lucky stones in my pockets and the lucky charms dangling from my handbag.

Life did not get easier for Nina or for us. So, when Nina was ten, I decided to try a two-pronged attack: I would seek help both through the school again *and* through the GP, and hope that at least one of them might come good.

I had a meeting with the school psychologist, a grey-haired woman who had somehow eluded me up to this point. Upon reading Nina's notes, she peered at me over her glasses and said, 'Please tell me you are claiming benefit?' I looked at her blankly. Er, no. Nina had no diagnosis, and it had never struck me I *could* apply for benefit, despite a regular working life being impossible.

As a result of this meeting, Nina was referred to the occupational therapist, and I was encouraged to buy pencil grips and fidget toys, which seemed a bit like rearranging the chairs on the Titanic and, of course, made no difference at all.

I was also sent on yet another parenting course held in the school.

I was fast becoming the best qualified mother in Midlothian.

This time, the strategy of the parenting course was time outs, which was the naughty step in a different guise. As usual, it was me and some other mothers who were trying to force their square-shaped children into round holes. There were also mothers who appeared to be struggling with alcohol or drugs, poverty or mental illness.

There were many problems represented in that room and time outs as even a partial solution to any of them was optimistic to say the least, but the course leader was nothing if not confident and declared: 'If you treat your child differently, you will have a different child.' I have quoted this enraging statement many times since, when trying to describe what parents of 'different' children are up against.

I eyeballed this *smug* young man and asked him, 'Do you

Sixteen

have children?' to which he replied, *smugly*, 'No, but my wife is pregnant.' The roomful of women waiting to be told how to be mothers replied in unison: 'Ahhh', and he drank in their goodwill. He continued: 'And whatever difficulties we may have, I will most certainly be using these same techniques to deal with them.'

I have thought about this young man, patting himself on the back, many times over the years, and although I would never wish hardship and difficulty on anyone, for him I may make a smug exception. 'Good luck,' I said at the time, insincerely, thinking, *just you wait*.

Most of the guidance I had been given over the years to help Nina deal with day-to-day life – ignoring her, sitting her on the naughty step, setting up star charts for rewards and time outs as punishments – had been techniques to basically bribe or shame her in order to 'retrain' her, and they had been ineffective. They had also been traumatic for us as parents and damaging to our relationship with Nina. They had been performative in the sense that it *appeared* we were getting help but in fact we were not – boxes were being ticked, but Nina's life was no easier.

During her art therapy, when she was seven, the therapist had noted that Nina painted a lot of red poppies and talked about *The Wizard of Oz*. It was the therapist's opinion that:

In the Wizard of Oz, of course, poppies make the gang feel so sleepy and wonderful that they don't realise they have been tricked. Although Nina was not able to link this with any of her own thoughts, feelings or behaviour, and although I did not draw her attention to it, I think the poppies are quite poignant as symbols of enticement to being controlled.

I recently asked Nina about this, and she commented: 'Maybe I just liked poppies.'

None of the suggested solutions had ever sat right with me, but over those ten difficult years, they were the only advice I could get. Despite our failed attempts to help her, Nina was still close to me. I knew she loved me, although sometimes I felt that she was drowning, clutching at me desperately even though I could not help. But she loved me, and she often showed it in little written messages. My silver locket has a scrap of paper in it that says: 'In all the world, there isn't a better mum.'

Unfortunately, the gentle parenting movement would not go mainstream for well over another decade. In 2025, it is getting millions of hits on social media. The idea of #gentleparenting is to 'enforce consistent boundaries with empathy, respect and understanding' and 'without shame, blame or punishment'. One gentle parenting advocate, clinical psychologist Becky Kennedy, says 'We are raising humans not animals'. This is a non-authoritarian approach, in which the parents look for the unmet need in the child and try to help.

Inevitably, there is a backlash against #gentleparenting, with claims that it creates mollycoddled brats and puts an intolerable strain on parents' own emotions, but surely it can't be harder on the parent or the child, or more ineffective than the 'solutions' I was offered from the previous era.

One family mealtime when the children were small, we were sitting down to eat, and I had just lifted my fork when Cello said something that implied that maybe it *was* my fault that we were struggling with Nina. Overtaken by blame-rage, I launched my fork across the table, as though I was throwing the school javelin, hitting the side of Cello's bowl, which dramatically broke clean in two.

As tomato sauce from the spaghetti leaked like blood onto the tablecloth, we all gazed at it. 'Well…' said Cello, 'there was

Sixteen

no need to do that to *my pasta*!' Whereupon he left the table without any dinner and retreated to the safety of his attic office.

Fortunately, the other prong to my attack – seeking help via the GP – did come good, and after several months on a waiting list, we were referred to a doctor – an actual fully-qualified medical doctor, lo and behold – at the Child and Adolescent Mental Health Service (CAMHS). We walked in and Nina immediately hugged Dr C and remarked, 'Oh, you smell nice,' and for once, I didn't feel the need to apologise or try to explain. If this woman, Dr C, did not understand Nina, then nobody would.

Dr C was friendly, welcoming, and seemed willing to listen, and within minutes of arriving, I felt we might get somewhere. I described how Nina could not fall asleep and she said, 'Oh, I can help with that,' and went on to explain that Nina's difficulty falling asleep was because she did not produce enough melatonin, which Dr C could prescribe in tablet form.

I blinked at her, hardly able to believe my ears. We had had ten years of Nina lying awake for hours on end every night, of her getting increasingly upset as the evening progressed because she believed that a lack of sleep would kill her, followed, inevitably, by me having to rouse her in the morning for school with both of us in a state of exhaustion and with me virtually dressing her myself – like a dead-weight rag doll – as she slept. I had told numerous doctors and therapists about this problem over the years, and discussed it with many psychologists and health workers, but had never got beyond the unhelpful suggestion of 'you must set a proper nighttime routine', and yet here was Dr C, unphased and confident that she could help.

'Do you mean she could get a proper night's sleep tonight?' I hardly dared to ask. Dr C smiled. 'Oh, yes,' she said, and it was as though she had parted the Red Sea and shown me the way to the Promised Land.

And indeed, that night Nina *did* take the melatonin and she *did* sleep right through the night for the first time since she was a baby, and we *did* feel we had witnessed a miracle. We were amazed and grateful and became devotees of Dr C.

'But you don't know the long-term effects of giving her melatonin!' declared another (unasked) mother, and I grimaced and thought, *Oh, do shut up*, but said, 'No, but I do know the short-term effects of having no sleep.'

Dr C had not flagged up any long-term negative effects, but even if she had, we certainly knew that there were long-term effects of sleep deprivation, which included a frightening litany of misery: stress, depression, obesity, diabetes, harmful effects on your immune system, plus memory and concentration problems, so we were willing to try melatonin. For other mothers – mothers on more straight-forward parenting journeys, mothers travelling along parenting highways not by-ways – using melatonin may have been considered too great a risk, but for us it was a risk we knew we had to take.

Life seemed so much easier for these other mothers who were not faced with the sorts of decisions that we had to make; mothers who nevertheless felt emboldened to comment no matter that they had no experience of such things. 'Smuggery' is how I thought of it. How much smuggery would I have cultivated if circumstances had been different? Perhaps if I had not had to negotiate the world as Nina's mum, I would have been self-righteous, smug and insufferable too. Perhaps I would have been one of those mothers who insisted that the reason their baby was able to fit in and co-operate was because they had managed their parenting right. Perhaps I too would have taken

Sixteen

the credit for my straightforward baby, thinking it was all my excellent parenting and not merely a stroke of good fortune.

This was painful, and the pain was converted into rage and fury. This furious, murderous anger – supressed, roiling, coiling anger – mixed with that kick-in-the-guts breathlessness at the lack of understanding from other mothers and at the injustice of it all, was a constant emotion in those days. Anger turned inwards; anger hidden because I'd rather have taken it out on myself than on Nina.

After several meetings with Dr C, she suggested Nina, who had just gone ten, should have an Autism Diagnostic Observation Schedule (ADOS) assessment for autism. As frightening as this sounded, knowledge is power, and we needed knowledge to be able to help Nina.

On the day, I took Nina to the clinic and sat with her while a specialist registrar asked her questions and got her to make up stories with dolls and other toys. Meanwhile, two consultant psychiatrists (including Dr C) watched from behind a two-way mirror. The specialist registrar was gentle and kind and Nina was happy, calm, and cooperative, and I wondered if these doctors were really seeing what they needed to see to make an assessment, seeing as she was not agitated, upset or overwhelmed, as was often the case.

The following week, Cello and I were invited back for the results. It sounds melodramatic but as we headed there, it felt like we had a date with destiny. This was something I had thought about a lot, something that should have happened years ago, but I was worried. What if they still could not tell us anything definitive? What if the tests were inconclusive? What if the experts left us twisting in the wind again? Or on the other hand, what if the tests were totally conclusive – how would what we were about to hear affect Nina's future? The world felt wobbly and unsafe: everything could change, or nothing could change, and I wasn't sure which was the more frightening.

Cello drove us the ten miles to the Sick Kids Hospital in Edinburgh, and I sat in the passenger seat in a state of high anxiety, feeling my stomach clench as I went into what felt like fight or flight mode.

In the clinic, Dr C got straight to the point. She said there had been agreement among all the doctors present at the assessment and they had concluded that Nina had Asperger's syndrome, which was a form of autism.

I could not speak and instead immediately burst into tears.

It was eight years since I had been officially told by the 'leading expert on autism in Scotland' that 'she does not have autism'; it was four years since I had been told 'she does not have a hard-wiring problem'; it was two years since I was told 'if you treat your child differently, you will have a different child'. Ten years of not really understanding her, blaming her for being her, showing frustration with her, being told all our troubles were my fault, feeling like such a failure, and now here was the explanation given in one simple sentence. Nina was autistic.

'You're not surprised, are you?' asked Dr C, clearly surprised herself at my reaction.

That was the moment I understood the previously puzzling phrase 'shocked but not surprised'. Despite all the years of being told otherwise, I had suspected this was the case, but was still shocked and deeply shaken that the official landscape of our lives had completely changed in the space of one sentence. I was frightened. What did Nina's future hold? Would she ever be able to find her niche in this world?

Sixteen

'What if she's right?' my sister had apparently once said to my mother, about my worries about Nina being different. 'What if Catherine is right and no one is listening?'

Now, at last, we had this information. Nina was the same girl she had always been – the diagnosis made no difference to that – but her whole context was different. We were now seeing her from an entirely new perspective. Previously, we had been trying to care for a Rolls Royce using the handbook of a Nissan Micra – now, at last, we could hopefully access the right information.

This diagnosis made sense of the intense level of parenting that had been required. All parenting is twenty-four seven, but my experience had been at such a high intensity, and now I had an explanation.

I had worried that the doctors would not appreciate Nina's difficulties during the assessment due to her being happy on the day, but I need not have feared. Dr C commented that seeing Nina in the assessment had highlighted just how much Nina struggled with certain communication and social skills, and she acknowledged that in the past, Nina had brought 'her considerable charm and articulate conversation to bear, which can mask her difficulties'. Dr C was at pains to remind us that Nina was still 'unique, engaging, interesting and charming' – something which we never doubted.

We decided that we would bring Nina to the clinic the following month so Dr C could explain the diagnosis to her.

A friend – a man who had previously told me he didn't believe ADHD existed – asked me a couple of days later, 'So have you got over your news?' This was a deeply stupid question, to which I could only splutter, 'Got over my news? I need to get over the preceding ten years first.'

Seventeen

As usual at times of crisis, I turned to books.

I read all I could about Asperger's syndrome, a term officially abandoned in 2013 and which is now covered by Autism Spectrum Disorder (ASD) – a term Nina dislikes because 'disorder' is a more stigmatising word than 'syndrome'.

I bought books online, books not usually found on the shelves of mainstream bookshops, books written from the viewpoints of boys with Asperger's and girls with Asperger's, with names like, *Standing Down...Falling Up*, *Freaks Geeks and Asperger's Syndrome*, and *Martian in the Playground*, books by parents of children with Asperger's and non-autistic experts on Asperger's.

I was desperate to understand as much about my child as possible. I bought books called *Asperger's Syndrome and High Achievement*, and *Natural Genius* – although whether they were to reassure Nina or to reassure me, I don't know.

I devoured these books, underlining, double underlining and highlighting as I went. The more I read, the more obvious Nina's autism became: the hypersensitivity to noise, smell, heat and touch; being able to detect individual odours of pedestrians in the street, and not perfumes or BO, but something much more fundamental, smells that were sometimes so lovely she took gulps as she passed and held them in. Being able to hear fluorescent lights, fans and fridges from the next room, and folding her ears over if a baby was crying or a lawnmower roaring anywhere nearby. Being able to smell the honey in a flower and the fruit in the wine but hating being at the service station because it reeked of petrol even inside the car. Being sensitive to the feel of zippers and waistbands, hating having her hair brushed and cut, hating being tapped on the shoulder and other unexpected touches, her discomfort in crowds and playing team sports.

I remembered the hyperlexia – the ability to decode letters very early. Her intense interests – 'special interests' – in dinosaurs, planets, times tables, *Pokémon* and so much more; her deep concentration that took her away from this world and into another; her agitation around change and transitions; her difficulty fitting in at school and making friends because other children could sense a difference. The tantrums she had had over the years, which I now understood to be autistic meltdowns – expressions of distress when the world had overwhelmed and overloaded her hypersensitive brain and could perhaps be better understood as a form of panic attack.

I wrote to her new class teacher at primary school and offered to lend her *Martian in the Playground* by Claire Sainsbury – a child's eye view of autism at school.

The teacher never replied.

Looking back, it seemed Nina had been presenting as a classic case of autism for years, so how had this diagnosis taken so long?

The 'leading expert on autism in Scotland' had sent us up a blind alley all those years ago. Supremely confident in his role as official know-it-all, and without expressing any doubts at all, he had robbed Nina of the help and support she needed. Looking back, I can't believe I wrote to thank him. Then, once up that blind alley, we had ricocheted from psychologist to psychologist for another eight years – psychologists who all had the same narrow vision and unbending, inappropriate advice, and whose sole purpose it seemed was to *make me make* Nina fit in, to *make her* the same as other children, to *make her* conform. In other words, to make me responsible for Nina's actions and to insist I got her to follow the rules to such a degree that she would fall into line and not cause anybody any inconvenience – at school or anywhere else for that matter – and in effect for me to make her not autistic at all.

The professionals, it seemed, had a fear of labelling children with a lifelong condition, although they didn't seem to mind labelling the parents as failed. However, if a condition is lifelong, surely it is better to understand it as early as possible, to help both the child and their parents. Self-knowledge can take a lifetime – some people travel the world to find it – so why deny it to autistic people? And how can autistic people get the support they need if they are not armed with all the information and the right terminology?

Somebody once said, 'we name in order to see better,' and putting a name to Nina's condition certainly made me see her better.

A year before her diagnosis, Nina had written her life story at school, which included the line 'I lead a normal life, but I am not normal myself'. How lonely that sounds. When I had asked her what she meant, she replied that she 'did not think' like other people.

Nina had known better than all of us, all along.

A month after the diagnosis, we revisited Dr C so she could tell Nina about the diagnosis. She opened the conversation by encouraging Nina to discuss her strengths, including 'focus' and 'determination', and her challenges, and then the doctor explained that she had seen other people with these same strengths and challenges and that they had something called Asperger's syndrome.

Nina listened intently and then suggested that this may be a topic of conversation with her classmates, but the doctor

Seventeen

advised caution and suggested she think about who might really need to know.

In the doctor's report, she said, 'Nina showed some interest in the diagnosis.'

But Nina was keeping much hidden from the doctor, and from us all.

Writing about this, four years later, Nina said, 'The first thing I did when I got home that day was burst into tears. I was autistic. I was cursed, tainted, diseased and soiled. I was a spaz, a mongo, a retard, a freak. And I would never get better.'

Sharing the diagnosis was a dilemma. Medical information is private and yet I wanted people who were involved in our day-to-day lives to understand her and to be kind to her. Some people who I mentioned it to treated it like gossip – repeating the information as though this wasn't my child's life they were talking about. 'Well, it's not a secret, is it?' they demanded, when I expressed concern. Well, no, but it's not for general chit-chat over a cup of tea either.

I sensed a gleeful excitement that I was having to deal with difficulties that they were not, and a sense of relief: 'Thank god it's you, not me'.

One of the advantages of us knowing that Nina was autistic was being able to 'explain' Nina to other people. I photocopied an information sheet produced by the National Autistic Society, *What to expect when you meet a person with autism*, which described 'potential challenges with communication and social interaction', and I sent it out with my Christmas cards that year. On the sheet, I wrote, 'I've included some simple info which may help when our paths cross over Christmas. Hopefully this may save on the explanations and apologies.'

I immediately received a reply from my old school friend, Carole, who said, 'Never feel that you have to explain or apologise for your children to me.'

Carole has a reputation for putting her foot in it in quite spectacular fashion – she once told an oral sex joke at a pre-wedding party before realising she was talking to the vicar – but this would not be the first nor the last time she would say exactly the right thing to me at exactly the right time.

Looking back now at the *What to expect when you meet a person with autism* information sheet, I know why I sent it – people did not understand autism and could be judgemental and unkind (they still can) – but it does make me wonder what would have been included on a 'What to expect when you meet a person without autism' information sheet, if one had been provided for Nina.

I recently asked Nina this question, and she suggested it might say 'Non-autistic people will be consistently loud, overbearing and will probably slightly bend their knees and then put their hands on their knees before looking down to talk to you. They will likely talk about the weather. They will express genuine surprise and shock at how intelligent and socially capable you are, and it will feel vaguely insulting.'

She pointed out that the message she always picked up from the non-autistic world was 'If a non-autistic person does not understand an autistic person, it is because the autistic person has poor communication skills. But if the autistic person does not understand a non-autistic person, it is because the autistic person has poor understanding.'

Which is a summary of a no-win situation that makes me want to cry.

Seventeen

'I can sympathise with you, but I cannot empathise,' said one unempathetic friend, trying to distance herself and her daughter from our situation, adding for absolute clarification: 'I personally have never experienced anything like this with my child.' Subtext: my child is brilliant and beautiful but, most importantly when it comes to fitting into the world, she is not like yours. She is *normal*.

Some of the perceived wisdom about autism puzzled me – a 'lack of empathy' was always mentioned and yet Nina could feel the pain of others very fiercely. As a five-year-old, she had approached the father of a crying toddler in Tesco to tell him he was 'a bad man' and she would like to 'blow him up with a bomb' for making the child cry. And yet a lack of empathy was one of the first things people *thought* they knew about autistic people.

Empathising, by putting herself in the shoes of the outsider, the underdog, the less powerful, was something Nina had always done and done very strongly – probably more strongly than most other people. She had a preoccupation with injustice and unfairness and, indeed, she could be described as hyper-empathetic.

She finds the suggestion that she has no empathy to be deeply hurtful, as well as inaccurate. 'People talk about autistic people as though they are psychopaths or sociopaths, which is just horrible.'

Other myths about autism came up again and again – the *Rain Man* stereotype being the most obvious. This was the idea that, like Dustin Hoffman's character in the 1980s film *Rain Man*, all autistic people were unable to live independently but were, simultaneously, maths geniuses.

What's her superpower? (Er…)
Is she really good at maths? (Well…)

Hold Fast

Ooh, I've heard of autistic savants. My dad once knew someone who could work out what day of the week you'd been born. (O-k-a-y...)

I looked back at my time employed as a fundraiser for autistic children when we milked the *Rain Man* stereotype for all it was worth (it had seemed too good an opportunity to miss) and I shuddered.

Lara was only seven, but we thought it was best to explain to her about Nina's Asperger's, so, as always, I got a book to read to her: *Brotherly Feelings: Me, my Emotions and my Brother with Asperger's Syndrome*. There was no corresponding 'Sisterly feelings about sisters with Asperger's syndrome'. We did not tell Nina about telling Lara. We were sensitive to Nina's privacy but also aware that Lara had to know.

It was hard to feel that you were doing right by them both.

Lara had never remarked on why it was that when they went to the corner shop together, we gave *her* the front door keys or the money to take care of rather than Nina, but Nina had noticed.

Nina, of course, being the elder one, had previously been used to being in charge around her younger sister. We have a video of them both aged around six and three years old in which they have set up a schoolroom in my bedroom. Nina is the teacher, and the pupils are an attentive cross-legged Lara who sits on the floor alongside a semi-circle of wilting teddies, knitted dolls and a stuffed pink elephant. Nina perches on my dressing table stool, ankles crossed, in a most teacherly fashion, and asks her pupils,

'And who can tell me the answer to two plus two?'

Lara's hand shoots up. Nina surveys the motely selection of toys as though she has not noticed Lara's hand.

Seventeen

'Elephant!' she says, leaning forwards, 'What do you think two plus two is? Four? Yes, four! Well done!'

She continues her lesson: 'And who can spell the word cat?'

Again, Lara's hand shoots up. Again, she is ignored.

'Teddy, what do you think?' asks Nina, looking studiously past a deflated Lara, her arm flagging.

And so it goes on; Nina the boss, Lara a bit-part – almost a no-part player in Nina's game.

Such is the powerful position of the elder child.

But once they had begun to leave the house without us, things had changed, and Lara had been the one given the responsibility, the one put in charge.

Nina said a long time afterwards that she thought she had never recovered from the undermining feeling of being infantilised in this way and added, 'It does not set up a person well to deal with adult life.'

Nina said that for years, she didn't know whether Lara knew about her autism or not, but very much had not wanted her to know because she was ashamed, whereas Lara remembered being told but never mentioned it to us again.

I realise now that we had done it wrong by not discussing it openly as a family. I had been trying to be sensitive but had only succeeded in implying to Nina that it was a taboo subject, and from her perspective, it looked as though I was shrouding the subject of autism in a shaming silence.

Lara has long joked she is 'The Forgotten Child' – a sentiment probably not uncommon in a family with a neurodivergent child. It didn't help that I kept getting her and the cat mixed up, culminating in Lara seeing in my diary 'do Lara's flea treatment'. The situation was made worse when I called her

'Kermit'. 'That's not even our cat!' she said, 'That's the neighbour's cat!'

Every time the 'Forgotten Child' gag reemerges, I assure Lara that she was not forgotten, never, not even for one moment, and she laughs and says it is only a joke – but it is a recurring joke that stirs a buried panic in me.

I have no memory of telling my mother about Nina's diagnosis. I must have done so, but my mother was in the process of dying of cancer at that time. Her cancer experience was a prolonged, traumatic and all-encompassing horror story that took over six years of a Snakes and Ladders, one-step-forward, two-steps-back journey of hope and terror and endless treatments – all of which seemed to make my mother's situation worse.

My mother's dying speeded up at the same time as Nina's autism diagnosis. In fact, the very week of Nina's diagnosis was the week my mother's non-Hodgkin lymphoma was declared terminal. It was a time of deep helplessness. It was later that week that I was squatting down in the garden with Cello standing beside me when he said, 'What's that?!' and I discovered I had a perfectly bald, pink patch on my scalp. I realised I had developed alopecia – my hair was falling out, as though my body was throwing up its hands and saying, *Oh, come on! Give me a break!* I didn't bother going to the doctor's about it – it would either grow back, or it wouldn't. I had bigger things to worry about just then.

One of the first people we asked for advice about Nina's diagnosis was a friend of Cello's, a former high-ranking SAS officer who had been involved in Operation Nimrod, the 1980 storming of the besieged Iranian Embassy, when (on live television)

Seventeen

members of the SAS abseiled from the embassy roof to rescue the hostages held within. We asked him, not because of his high calibre Special Services work, but because he had also raised a non-neurotypical child.

We met up in an Italian restaurant. He was a big man squeezed behind a small table and was carrying a briefcase from which he took out a handwritten list of tips, neatly scribed in capitals. His list began:

- Start a File.

So, I did: an A4 clip file that over the years morphed into two bulging Lever Arch files with sections including Occupational Therapy, Other therapies, Letters to MPs, School Outreach Worker, Consultant Psychiatrist and Benefits. So much about trying to help a non-neurotypical child is the paperwork, searching for information, handling information and keeping records.

The SAS officer's list was long but also included:

- Read everything on autism – and keep reading.

(This was one lesson I didn't need encouragement to learn.)

- Talk to as many experts and people with similar experiences as possible – and keep talking.
- Large gatherings may be a problem – avoid them, but not altogether.

And one, further down, which could possibly be as difficult as abseiling down the besieged Iranian Embassy:

- Never lose your temper or shout.

Over the years, other people's input and comments were less helpful:

'I used to work with someone with Asperger's. His mother was so pleased by the time I'd finished with him because he could pour tea when they had visitors.'

'I don't know how you cope…'
'I've always dreaded having an autistic child…'
'I think we're all a bit autistic though…'
'We're all a bit spectrum-y aren't we?' (Er, no: the term 'spectrum' conveys the idea that autism can manifest in many ways, in different people, not that it covers everyone.)
'My friend's son is autistic, *but* he is lovely…'
…but…
…but…
That 'but'.

We try to explain the difficulties and challenges faced by those with autism in this non-autistic world, and sometimes you feel like you are getting through, but at other times it is as though people don't have the ears to hear. There are many veils between those who know, those who live it, those who live with it, and those who do not.

Again, it makes me ponder how unknowing I am of other people's experiences; how I too must blunder through the world ignorant of the challenges others face, putting my foot in it and causing offence as I go.

Eighteen

I glance through my old address book from the dark days of pre-diagnosis and I see listed there a series of dead ends and dashed hopes, a catalogue of failure, frustrations and false starts, some of which still feel like a kick in the guts: cranial massage therapists, speech and language therapists, school psychologists, key workers, counsellors, lists of Nina's friends – some of whom became her tormentors – 'advocacy for education' and parent helplines. And mixed in amongst all these futile numbers are other numbers relating to my little sister, Tricia, who was suffering from bipolar disorder at the same time: crisis teams and care coordinators, duty teams and consultant's secretaries, out-of-hours emergency numbers, and yet more key workers, and lurking alongside those numbers are the numbers for my mother's cancer specialists. It's no wonder I began to dread the sight of that address book and, eventually, had to throw it in the bin and get another.

I went along to various support groups for families of children with autism, but I did not find my tribe. The other parents seemed to be dealing with children disabled in different ways – children who were incontinent, children who were nonverbal, children who were attending special schools, children who had often received an autism diagnosis when they were very young and without the parents having to fight for it, and whose conditions manifested very differently. Understandably, their priorities were often not the same as mine – mainly setting up respite weeks during school holidays – so my membership of these groups petered out.

Hold Fast

We were advised by Dr C to find a trusted babysitter and make sure that Cello and I got out on our own every now and then, and this seemed to be the best advice. We would eat a curry at the local Indian restaurant, being fussed over by the charming Mohammed, but for a lot of the time sitting in a stunned silence. But it was a silence we valued, and to us more helpful than a support group.

On my fortieth birthday – when Nina and Lara were nine and six years old – we had dared to book a couple of days away for just me and Cello. We chose Copenhagen because the flight was so short that we could be boarding the plane in Edinburgh at six o'clock in the morning and sitting on the hop-on hop-off bus in Copenhagen city centre by ten.

I had had two big dreams about what I wanted to achieve by the time I hit forty – an age that felt like a landmark birthday. I had wanted to have children and to have written a book. The writing a book dream had all but withered by then, but I had certainly achieved the children.

It was, however, lovely to be without them for a couple of days. Cello and I visited the Erotica Museum just because we could – *because we had no children with us*.

A childless state was difficult to credit and something to be temporarily relished.

A neighbour I barely knew had stopped me not that long before as I walked to the shops in my hometown, and he had remarked, 'This is the first time I have ever seen you out and about not pushing that buggy!'

In the Erotica Museum, we wandered around the exhibits of erotic art, sexual aids in glass cases, and walls covered in framed *Playboy* covers, trying to look grown up and not titter like the group of young Japanese men ahead of us.

Afterwards, we headed to Copenhagen's main art gallery.

Eighteen

We gawped up and down the street, guidebook in hand, and Cello said, 'I think that might be it,' and we both gazed up at a grand building bearing the legend 'Museum for Kunst'.

We started laughing. We could not stop laughing. I could hear my mother's voice telling me 'Catherine, do not be so *puerile*!' But I could not stop. I knew this was juvenile, but I laughed so hard, bent double, stomach muscles hurting, tears running down my face, that I thought I might melt into the Copenhagen pavement.

How wonderful it was to be out and about in an adult world, acting like children. How wonderful it was to be partners for a short time, rather than parents.

We had left Cello's brother Rino and his mother Rosa in charge at our house. It wasn't until we returned home that we discovered Nina and Lara had been messing with the phones in Cello's office while we were gone and had succeeded in phoning a random lady, who asked them what they were doing and was told they were alone because their parents had gone on holiday without them. A few minutes later, Rino and Rosa – the world's most dedicated and careful babysitters – had received a call from the police: 'We have received a report that young children at this address have been left at home unattended…'

Nina still hated school. The sexism was one of the things that upset her. When the class was studying the ancient Romans, she remembers one of the boys making a badge with what he thought was the symbol for Mars on it – the symbol for the God of War, military power and 'the noise and blood of battle'. When Nina pointed out that in fact he had used the symbol of a circle and a cross rather than a circle and an arrow and therefore his badge was *actually* the symbol for

Venus – the goddess of love and beauty – he threw his work on the floor in disgust and refused to touch it.

Another of the boys at school was particularly horrible to Nina, insulting her and calling her names, trying to get a laugh at her expense. He picked on her curly hair, her supposed 'masculine' appearance, her 'nerdy' interests. This kind of behaviour is sometimes trivialised as teasing – the implication being that it is being done in a playful way and must therefore be accepted in the same spirit. It wasn't. It was isolating, undermining and bullying, and all the more difficult to deal with when disguised as a bit of fun.

It is hard to know how to handle these situations when they happen so often and leave you feeling you are fighting fires on all fronts, while, at the same time, you are desperate to keep the school on your side.

Lara once found a friend crying in the girls' toilets because she had complained to a teacher that she was being picked on and 'teased', and the teacher had told her that perhaps it was *her* fault and maybe she ought to try harder to make herself more likeable. Oddly, the teacher involved was one of the teachers who I had always admired because he had been good with Nina.

Schools are complicated and dangerous environments for vulnerable children.

At one school event, I was sitting in the audience beside another mother from Nina's class, who mentioned a particular boy's name and said he had been bullying her daughter. I told her that boy had been horrible to Nina too. We were discussing our experiences when a third mother, seated in the row in front, turned and berated us for discussing this bullying boy. 'He is a child! You shouldn't be saying these things!'

Eighteen

It was as though she had lit the blue touch paper, but unfortunately for her she had not immediately stood back, and the second mother and I detonated in her face. In unison, we exploded: 'How dare you tell me not to talk about my daughter's experiences!' It was an explosion caused by the sheer frustration of having your child bullied, feeling that you are helpless, and then being told you can't even talk about it. We raged at her: 'Don't tell me what I can say about my daughter being bullied!'

My fury was so intense I felt I might levitate from my seat. The third mother, realising her mistake too late, turned and faced resolutely forward, desperately trying to maintain her foothold on the moral high ground, as her teenaged daughter smiled at us apologetically over her shoulder.

One day, Cello was picking Nina up from primary school and was waiting in the yard when another pupil from Nina's class started squirting water at him from behind. He told her to stop and asked her to get her mum or dad to phone him later. He then went in to see the deputy head about Nina and when he mentioned what had happened, the depute said, 'Oh, we have a problem then,' and went on to explain that no other parents were allowed to talk to that particular girl. Cello had to stop himself from combusting and said, 'So she's squirting me with water, and I'm not allowed to tell her to stop?'

It seemed so.

Sometimes we felt we were not sending Nina to school but sending her through the looking glass.

Nina was now receiving support from the Autism Outreach Service, which involved a young woman I will call Anne coming into school to sit with Nina with the aim of explaining what Asperger's syndrome was and discussing the many ways it may impact her life.

Anne immediately embarked on lessons in anger management.

There was no discussion about why Nina might feel justifiably angry; no acknowledgment that ten years of being misunderstood, of feeling out of step, being blamed, rejected, scapegoated and made to feel like an outsider, of being berated for being a fish out of water, of having people implying that something was wrong with her and making her feel like she was a failure, of her trying to survive in what must have felt like a hostile environment while being treated as if she was a puzzle to be solved or a problem to be fixed would make *anyone* feel angry.

Nina had wanted the world to say, 'we accept you', but at school, the opposite had happened, and she had been rejected.

Anne encouraged us to hang a punch bag in the playroom to 'release some energy', which we did, but I never saw Nina use it. Anne told Nina that she would get greater respect from her peers if she was 'assertive' rather than 'aggressive' – a somewhat moot point when you are ten years old and being picked on, taunted and ostracised by classmates.

If these things were happening, suggested Anne, and Nina felt upset or angry, perhaps instead of biting herself, she could use a stress ball?

Years later, Nina explained that anger had felt better than sadness or resignation, which had seemed to her to be the only alternatives. She had no way of articulating this at the time, but she felt that anger had been a means of survival, and so she did not want to be trained out of it.

In one of her reports, Anne said Nina's autistic 'rigid way of thinking' became apparent quite soon. As an example, she cited Nina saying, 'My ambition is to do well in all aspects of life, and I think I'll achieve it.' Years later, on discovering this report, Nina objected and said, 'Maybe my "rigid thinking" was *rational*.

Eighteen

When does a "rigid thinker" become a "person of conviction"?'

It's a fair question. Would a non-autistic child have been accused of 'rigid thinking' for stating they wanted 'to do well in all aspects of life'? I think not, and nor should they be. A ten-year-old autistic girl with confidence was apparently a threat to be neutralised. Why, when something is associated with autistic people, does it automatically become a negative?

Likewise, an autistic person's 'special interest' is never described as a 'passion' – a term that sounds wholly positive and means 'something that makes life worth living'. More likely, their special interest will be portrayed as an obsession and something to be controlled, and possibly even removed as a punishment.

Newly diagnosed, Nina was taken out of class to fill in sheets identifying her emotions. As she also pointed out years later, in all the time she was at school, none of the pupils who were horrible to her were ever taken out of class and sat down with a sheet and asked to identify *their* feelings and emotions.

She said: 'It was never the kids who called me a retard because I was socially different from them and got help from the learning support department, or the kids who kicked me who were segregated. It was never them who were put into therapy to try to promote their empathy. They were never the ones given anti-depressants. Why?'

All the responsibility was put on the autistic child to 'get better at social situations' rather than the responsibility being put on the other kids to stop picking on her.

Twenty years later, I sift through the paperwork from her outreach sessions with Anne at primary school. One week's session was a worksheet entitled *Do you Attract New Friends Easily?*, which asked:

Are you too keen, too soon? Do you act needy? Do you want too much to be liked? Do you reveal too much too quickly? Are you negative? Do you bad-mouth others? Are you always complaining? Moaning and groaning? Criticising? Putting others down? Do you think you are the greatest? Do you show off? Do you compete in a conversation? Do you always want your own way? Are you boring? Too obsessed with a single topic? Do you give too much detail? Do you take too long to get to the point? Do you talk about topics of no interest to other people? Are you a fraud? Do you tell lies? Do you pretend to be what you are not? Are you shut off? Do you not tell others much about yourself? Are you insensitive? Do you tell others' secrets? Are you greedy? Unreliable? Unhelpful?

Reading this, twenty years after the event, each question feels like a judgemental kick in the guts. This is a questionnaire that would be hard-going for an adult, let alone a distressed ten-year-old, currently being bullied, who had just officially been declared to be different.

Then I notice that Nina had completed a self-assessment sheet on the above questions. She had put a tentative question mark next to 'Do you talk about topics that have no interest for the other person?' but on the whole, she had scored well and had fallen into the category of 'You probably attract people fairly easily'. Beside this, Anne had written 'But Nina feels that is not true.'

Next in these outreach sessions, I discover another brutal questionnaire: *How Interesting are You?* This one asks:

Do you give too much detail in a story? Do you make sure other people are interested? Do you get to the point quickly? Do you check every now and then that the other person is still interested? Do you repeat yourself? Do you use a variety of voice tones?

Then I note with horror that *I* was asked to take part in this

Eighteen

questionnaire. I have no memory of it, but it is undeniably my handwriting filling in the form: 'Nina can get very technical with *Sims* stuff,' I wrote, 'but shows great enthusiasm.' 'Nina is very well-informed and witty, therefore is interesting to talk to. I would like her to talk more and relax about it.' 'Nina gets a bit upset if anyone interrupts her story, she tends to lose her thread.' 'Nina is a very animated conversationalist. More smiles and laughs needed!!'

I am relieved I was positive but gutted that I took part in what must have felt like an exercise in potential character assassination to Nina.

On another of her outreach worksheets, it was printed: 'My mum and dad want me to learn about autism so that I know I am a special and wonderful person.' But saying the words 'a special and wonderful person' doesn't help if the whole exercise is not making the participant feel either special or wonderful, but more like a freak.

The expectation to make Nina fit in and, in effect, not act like she was autistic at all, appeared to have passed from my shoulders to hers.

One week, Anne asked Nina what she was frightened of, and she replied, 'I'm worried when I fail.'

I wonder where she had picked up that familiar way of thinking?

Unsurprisingly, looking back, Nina was upset after her meetings with Anne. After weeks of learning how different she was and all the many ways she could mess up the daily interactions that, apparently, were straightforward for everyone else, Nina wrote plaintively on the bottom of her worksheet: 'I don't want to read about my way of thinking.' She told me, 'I never want to see her again. If you think that I'm a lunatic, then put me in a loony bin.'

But rather than seeing this from Nina's point of view, I was so grateful to be receiving *any* so-called help from *anyone* that I didn't question their expertise, or the wisdom of their approach. Instead, I clung on and hoped for the best.

Hindsight is a wonderful thing.

Anne was very keen on things called 'social stories' (trademarked).

In the deadening, stultifying, language of such things, social stories were described as 'a social learning tool that supports the safe and meaningful exchange of information between parents, professionals, and people with autism of all ages'.

Through my layman's eyes, they were simple stories about day-to-day events written in first-person as though composed by the autistic person themselves. Again, years later, Nina and I looked with horror at the social stories she had been given at primary school.

One was entitled *A story about Social Accidents* and began, 'At school, most children are kind most of the time. Children try to be friendly and helpful.'

Well, that may be the experience of *some* children, but it certainly wasn't the experience of Nina. Children aged ten sense difference and try to distance themselves from it. Nina was very aware of this and did her best to blend in, believing that the other children thought being different was 'a stupid thing'. But despite her attempts to blend in, far from most children being kind, Nina was often left out, or became the butt of jokes and insulting remarks. Other children – supposed friends – would walk to school with her but told her to not to interact with them once inside school.

The social story goes on: 'when people bump into each other…this is NOT people being nasty…'

Eighteen

Well, maybe, or maybe not.

Looking back on these social stories, they appear to be one gigantic gaslighting exercise; they are as good as saying: *Do not believe the evidence of your own ears. Do not believe the evidence of your own eyes. Do not trust your gut instinct.*

In fact, Nina's experience was: 'At school, many children are not kind most of the time. Some children are spiteful and unhelpful.' Maybe if the social stories had acknowledged the truth of the situation, rather than denying it, they would have been more helpful.

As Nina puts it, social stories were 'an ableist and coercive method to convince autistic people that they were responsible for how badly they were treated'. And she felt that the message behind the system was 'Be nicer!' It's your fault! You don't try! Try harder! Try better!'

Finding out you are autistic and then being told that what you think you are experiencing is not actually what you *are* experiencing is enough to make anyone doubt their own sanity.

I regret not questioning these social stories at the time. They seemed an over-complicated way to achieve very little, but it was as though I believed there *must be* some magical ingredient in them that I didn't quite grasp but that I *must trust* and all would be well.

Well, I did trust, and all was not well.

Nineteen

At high school, Nina's struggle to fit in intensified. There was much talk from the transition team about setting up something called a buddy scheme where she would be partnered up with an older child to support her – but nothing ever materialised.

In trying to reassure her that everything would be fine, I felt we had again been gaslighting her. I found a note in her bedroom: 'All my relatives who said high school would be challenging and fun have lied to me.'

Twice in the early days of high school, we had to scour the local area to find her because she had run away, believing she had been told off.

She did not want any of the children to know about her autism diagnosis and came home distraught one day when some paperwork had been handed out in class to each pupil and Nina's baldly stated on the front: Has Nina a disability? YES.

She tried to camouflage her autism – to mask her true self, to appear to be the same as everyone else, to be normal, to be accepted, maybe even popular. She wanted to be one of the 'scary girls' so she asked for expensive designer hoodies (which we bought) and £100 trainers (which we didn't buy at first but eventually did), and she wanted to wear dark foundation and got her curly hair straightened. This was a job I did every morning while she ate her breakfast – after I'd struggled her into her uniform as she sat up in bed still more or less comatose because despite the melatonin, Nina remained sleep-deprived.

One morning as I straightened away, worrying about what fresh horror school would bring today, I felt a fluttering in my chest. It got worse; I could not ignore it. I began to gasp for breath and went to hang over the back of the sofa. My heart was bouncing under my ribs. I phoned the GP: 'I think I'm having a heart attack.' 'Well, I suppose you'd better come in then,' replied the underwhelmed receptionist.

In the surgery, I was wired up to a monitor. 'Ooh, we don't normally have people coming in who are still having the symptoms,' said the doctor, looking perky, as though this was quite an interesting start to his day. However, a while later, he said, 'It's all regular,' and I looked at him in disbelief, so he showed me the heart trace, which did indeed look as regular as clockwork. 'But I can still feel it!' My heart was still tugging and jumping in my chest. Except it wasn't – the evidence said so. Despite feeling like I was going to die, I was, it seemed, having a panic attack.

When I told a friend that I had been diagnosed with panic attacks, they said, 'What have you got to be anxious about?'

So, my perfect life act must have been convincing somebody, at least.

Nina's attempts to be the same as everyone else failed because even when she looked like the other girls, she knew she 'didn't act, speak or think like them'. She was clever, she always got top marks and was keen to keep them that way to 'have a good future'. Her favourite subjects of conversation remained politics and current affairs, so she was labelled 'posh' or 'stuck-up'. When the girls gathered round her in the girls' changing rooms to ask how many boyfriends she'd had and she said she'd had none, they shrieked with laughter, which she remembers 'ringing round the tiled walls'.

She wrote a letter to the deputy head telling him it was an injustice because when people picked on her, the teachers never noticed but when she retaliated, they did notice, and so it was her that got into trouble. She said, 'I wish there was a school for clever people, where everyone wanted to learn and didn't make childish personal comments about other kids. I'd want to go there. I wish they would build one.'

She was incredibly bright and creative, and yet her school reports made depressing reading: 'Nina…finds it difficult to participate…finds it difficult to focus…finds it difficult to follow instructions…does not always do what the task requires…does not mix…could have achieved more…finds it difficult to listen…'

It seemed to be up to us, her parents, to come up with the solutions. I suggested that the teachers wrote any instructions down on the board rather than give them out verbally. Surely this would benefit the other children too?

PE lessons were a huge stress for Nina; the sports hall was loud and echoey and team sports were unpredictable and hostile. Taking part in the lessons involved quick changes of uniform in the changing room – a task she found tricky in yet another environment she found hostile. Nina now believes she has dyspraxia – a condition that affects physical co-ordination and is often co-morbid with autism, which obviously made things even more difficult. Although it wasn't that she was physically unfit – hours spent on the trampoline and playing outdoors kept her fit. Her dislike of PE lessons was not helped by the Scottish country dancing lesson in which all the girls were lined up in the middle of the hall and the boys told to choose who they would like to dance with – an arrangement that seemed gratuitously humiliating for the girls.

As homework continued to cause friction at home because Nina thought it unfair to continue schoolwork once she was home (I sympathised), I suggested to the school that she opt

Nineteen

out of PE lessons and instead complete her homework sitting in the Special Needs Base during those lessons.

Schools are not renowned for their flexibility, and it took me the whole of the first year to persuade the school (first tentatively, then more forcefully) that this was a good idea – despite this being a simple bit of rule bending with no additional costs to the school. Once in place, in the second year, it worked perfectly, and as far as I was concerned, killed two birds with one stone.

When I complained to a friend that getting the right support was hard, he snapped, 'Schools can't make adjustments for *everyone*! There are thirty children in each class – *everybody* has *something*.' To which I replied, 'Would you expect a blind pupil not to have adjustments made?' And he rolled his eyes.

In raising my family, other people's problems have rarely been my problems.

I remember a mother putting her hand up at an open meeting at the high school and saying, 'Our Kyle doesn't seem to be getting much homework,' and I looked around to see which mad woman was speaking. Do some people have so few problems that they have to go looking for them?

At all times, I was aware that I needed to keep the school on side. My child was vulnerable; she was in the power of the school authorities and away from my protection all day. It was essential that I co-operate with them as much as I could and show that I appreciated any help they gave me. This was a very disempowering position. I was constantly on the back foot, apologetic, thankful.

Nina was allocated a key worker at high school who would email me details of the homework Nina had been doing during the day, and I always emailed back to say 'thank you', to show her that her efforts were appreciated. Some time later, it was reported back to me, by a senior member of the school staff, that I was 'inundating the keyworker with emails'. I felt hurt and humiliated as it was not acknowledged that these emails were mainly emails of thanks.

It was difficult to avoid the feeling that you were considered a difficult parent of a difficult child. For someone like me who had been brought up with the belief that to be a nuisance and to ask for things – anything – was unacceptable, to be the parent of a child with a disability is especially uncomfortable. But you have no option: no matter how difficult it is, you must keep on asking for things.

After my intensive reading and research about Asperger's, I began to see autism everywhere – the child who was described as 'difficult', 'awkward', 'in a world of her own', 'one of her own', 'walking to the beat of their own drum', 'a bit weird'; children who were shunned or ridiculed by other children; children who other mothers pursed their lips at with a 'that spoilt child needs a good hiding' look; children who lost themselves in books and computer games. I felt drawn to them and protective of them.

One day, I was volunteering in Lara's class at the primary school and saw a boy who it seemed obvious to me had Asperger's syndrome. He was lining up to borrow one of twenty different maths sacks – bags of maths-based puzzles and numbers, all of which had different themes. I could see that this little boy, who was sixth in the queue, was getting desperately anxious in case the maths sack he wanted, on the theme of trains, got chosen before he got there. It appeared that the children ahead of him couldn't care less if they had this maths sack, that maths sack, or no maths sack at all. I whispered to the classroom assistant that maybe we could put

Nineteen

the train maths sack aside for him to cut down on his anxiety as he waited. It was obvious what a big difference that would make to him, probably for the rest of the day, possibly for the rest of the week. But the classroom assistant drew herself up to her full five foot three, pursed her lips and hissed, 'We are all equal here. Nobody gets special treatment.'

As so often, I was lost for words, and I gaped at her. Yes, indeed, Miss Five-Foot-Three, we are all of equal value, but that does not make all our needs the same.

Twenty

As Mum ailed, we visited her as often as we could, while also being aware that she found it stressful having too many people around for too long. One day while staying with her, I took Nina and Lara for a walk up the lane and we picked wildflowers from the hedgerows. I realised that besides the obvious buttercups and daisies, I knew very few of their names. Late in life, Mum had done a City and Guilds qualification in flower arranging and she had loved it; in fact, I think those flower arranging classes were the happiest times of her life.

I thought this might be a good opportunity for her to tell Nina and Lara the names of the flowers we had picked as they pressed them into a scrapbook. It had always appeared that Mum enjoyed being a grandmother more than she had enjoyed being a mother. She was relaxed with her five grandchildren in a way she had not been with me and my sisters.

Mum was sitting in the conservatory when we got back with a carrier bag full of flowers.

'What is the name of this?' I asked pulling a leaf out of the tangle.

'I don't know,' she said.

'How about this?' I pulled out another.

'Oh, stop mithering,' she snapped, flapping her hand at me. I hastily withdrew.

I thought that seeing the end of her life approaching, she might have been keen to create memories with her grandchildren, but I had over-estimated her patience and under-estimated the trauma of dying from cancer.

I made sure that was the last time she told me to stop mithering.

Twenty

One day, a few months later, several years into her cancer diagnosis, I phoned my mother, and she could not form words, only gobbledygook. Dad took the receiver and all he could say was, 'I don't know, I don't know…' and it was clear she was near the end.

In June 2006, on her penultimate night, I slept on a camp bed beside her deathbed – which seemed to loom overhead in the darkness. The night was black, velvety and dense, like only a country night can be. I lay awake until the sunrise eked a thin grey light across the fields and into the room. I put a cushion under her calves to stop her heels getting pressure sores and gave her the odd sip of water. It was hard to grasp that within hours, my mother would be gone; a world without a mother was a strange and unimaginable thing.

That night, she was put on a morphine driver, which upset Dad because he knew that morphine spelled the end and he wanted to put the end off as long as possible. Perhaps if we didn't face up to it, it would never happen?

My sister Elizabeth was in the camp bed that last night and came to wake us all at 5am. 'I think you'd better come.' Dad and Elizabeth held her hands, and Tricia and I perched on the end of the bed. She opened her eyes briefly to look around at us all, then closed her eyes and took her last breath.

Sometime later, Elizabeth told me that towards the end, Mum had told her: 'My life would have been nothing without you three.'

Cello and the children arrived the day after from Edinburgh. It was a surreally hot summer, and the World Cup was on. Cello was desperate to watch the Italy versus Germany semi-final and was grabbing bags from the car. In his haste to get to the televised match, he fell down the cattle grid – both legs up to the kneecaps – the same cattle grid he had spent the past ten years warning: 'Somebody's going to fall down that bloody cattle grid one of these days.'

Meanwhile, we were in the back garden; my nephews, Chris and Kieran, polishing their shoes for the next day's funeral. 'What's that noise?' asked someone. 'A bird,' answered someone else, until the far distant anguished cries for help became clearer and we dropped polish and brushes and shot round the house.

Cello had all his weight on his right knee (his football kicking knee, which must have been a bit bigger). Chris and Kieran hauled him out and helped him into the house, where he sat on the sofa clutching a packet of frozen peas to his kneecaps.

Dad watched the match with him, and as play got into the final minute and Italy scored, Cello dropped the peas, leapt from the sofa, punched the air and did a lap of the living room, yelling, 'Yes! Yes! What a goal!'

Dad, widowed only a matter of hours, burst out laughing and said, '*He's* soon recovered.'

Cello apologised, and Dad shook his head and said, 'Margaret would have enjoyed that.'

The girls wrote notes to put in my mother's coffin. I asked Lara recently what she wrote on the note, and she said that she couldn't remember that, but she 'could still hear the noise' of Cello stuck in the cattle grid.

I asked Cello what he recalled of that day, and he said, 'It was nil nil, approaching the end of extra time, and I knew you don't beat Germany in a penalty shootout, then in the 119th minute they scored a magnificent goal...The relief was overwhelming...Ah...happy days,' and he smiled reminiscently, before adding, 'apart from your mother dying, of course.'

Twenty

A little later, he clarified: 'The moment that goal went in was the greatest surge of pure joy – zero to 100 – of my whole life.'

A few months later, I said to Elizabeth: 'My life is easier without a mother,' and she recoiled. 'What would she say if she heard you say that?' And I shuddered at the thought.

Where had that sentiment come from? I hadn't known I was going to say it until it came out, but having verbalised it, I recognised it as being true.

I had always felt a lot of responsibility for my mother's happiness, and yet found it almost impossible to make her happy. Being expected to do something without knowing how, and always failing, is hard. It had become harder and harder as she slowly died of cancer and the guilt and feelings of helplessness had hung heavy.

After she died, and those feelings lifted, it was only then that I realised how crushing they had been.

Twenty-One

I heard on the grapevine that Nina's high school was holding an awards evening.

There had been no official notification nor any mention anywhere else about this ceremony. Nina was clever; she was diligent and hardworking and she always got top marks, and yet she had not been invited. I phoned the school and asked why. The woman on the phone seemed a bit non-plussed to be asked this question so directly. 'Because the teachers haven't given her an award,' she replied. Which wasn't really answering my query. Why hadn't they given her an award when she produced amazingly creative work, tried so hard, and had to use a hundred times more courage than most kids just to get out of bed and go to school at all? But answer came there none.

What was particularly galling was that with Nina's drive to do well, an awards ceremony may have boosted her damaged confidence and made her feel accepted and as though she belonged at the school. Whereas a few years later when Lara was at the high school and was being invited to every awards evening going, she didn't give two hoots. 'Do we have to go?' Awards were easy come, easy go to Lara.

I went to Lara's awards ceremonies with her, despite her boredom with them. Did we have to go? Yes, yes we did! Having been excluded with Nina, I wanted to experience the school as a 'have' parent rather than a 'have not'. I felt annoyed all over again that the school's resources (I presumed) were being spent on these glasses of wine and strawberry tarts for the (mainly) middle-class kids and middle-class parents in attendance; the same kids who received plaudits every day of the week because they fitted in and found school life easy.

Twenty-One

Where were the pupils with different challenges, how many of those pupils were here? Not many, I guessed.

The speaker at one of Lara's awards ceremonies was a local girl done good, a former pupil at the school, a hairdresser by royal appointment who had worked with many members of the royal family and had become a successful businesswoman. She gave a talk about leaving school with few qualifications but not letting that stop her making her dreams come true. She underlined that you did not need to be an academic high-flyer or to go to university to become the very best at what you do.

She was an interesting and entertaining speaker, but surely it was the kids who *weren't* planning to go to university who would have benefitted most from her inspiring talk; the kids who weren't academic book learners with school awards coming out of their ears. The kids whose 'teachers had not given them an award', the kids who weren't here.

As I balanced my glass of white wine and strawberry tart, I challenged the headteacher, a vast man who exerted authority with his large physical presence and booming voice and who didn't like to be questioned. What about the non-award winners who would be more likely to be inspired by this speaker as a role model? Why were they missing out on this opportunity? The polite smile slid down his jowls, and he glared at me. The speaker, he said, 'may' be able to visit again sometime to go around the classrooms to see 'the others'.

And then he turned on his heel.

Nina found the corridors at the high school noisy and stressful, so Dr C suggested she take her iPod to school to use while getting from one classroom to another. We knew Nina was being picked on at school and so we were not very surprised when her iPod went missing within a day or two. I phoned the school and asked the receptionist politely if the school could keep an eye out for it. I was not asking them to do a search. I was not criticising anyone or demanding anything. A few moments later, I got an outraged phone call from the vast headmaster, at full volume: 'iPods were banned in school!' he boomed. 'Why had she brought an iPod to school? Did you not know this was against the rules?'

I explained about the psychiatrist. If that was the case, he demanded, why had I not informed the school of this advice? That was a good question. Why hadn't I? Because the thought had never crossed my mind? Because it didn't occur to me that we would get any help or cooperation whatsoever, no matter what the psychiatrist suggested? Because I thought helping Nina to survive at school was *our* job – not theirs, because that is how it always felt, because that is how *he* had made it feel. He continued to bellow down the phone until I was crying too much to answer, at which point I put the phone down.

The following day, a furious Cello went into school first thing and asked for a meeting with the head and the deputy. 'Why did I get home last night to find my wife crying?' The headmaster apparently looked a little taken aback, but repeated his assertion several times that iPods were against the rules. He lifted the book of school rules and brought it down with a bang onto the table between them and kept crashing it down at intervals until Cello took it and flung it on the desk behind him.

As parents, we were clearly getting nowhere trying to deal with those in positions of power.

A few days later, the iPod was discovered on a high wall. It had not been taken because anyone wanted it – it was bright pink so not everybody's cup of tea, and anyway was easily identifiable – it had been taken out of badness.

Twenty-One

The thought of being meaningfully helped by 'the authorities' – the school, medics, social services anyone besides Dr C – was a million miles away, and this situation came into sharp focus one evening when Nina was twelve and Lara nine.

Cello had interviewed the serial killer Archie 'Mad Dog' McCafferty for the *Sunday Times* and several times again over the years as a freelance journalist.

Archie was born in Scotland and was taken to Australia as a child. When his baby son died in tragic circumstances, a drugged-up Archie came to believe his son would be resurrected if he murdered seven people. He murdered three before being imprisoned in 1974, and another while in prison. Upon release in 1997, he was deported back to Scotland, where his Wikipedia entry described him as 'the Australian Charles Manson'.

Following Cello's interviews, he became a friend of ours. He came to the house and met the children, bringing with him one of his paintings as a gift: a gecko in the style of an Aboriginal dot painting. Nina remembers him as 'grizzled but friendly'. She says she 'only got suspicious' when he refused to tell her why he had left Australia despite rhapsodising about the place.

Cello wrote what was supposed to be a feel-good piece for a tabloid newspaper about how Archie was a reformed man who was now in a loving relationship with his Scottish girlfriend. Within hours, the social services had knocked on his girlfriend's door and removed her two young children.

When I heard about these children being removed from their beds that night and taken goodness know where – despite Archie never having committed crimes against children, or sexual crimes – I was beside myself with fear. What was to stop them coming to our house and taking our children? Archie was a friend; he had spent time here with them.

'Lock the door!' I said. 'Turn the lights out!' No matter who came, they were not getting in. They would take my children over my dead body. The idea that any contact with the social services could be good contact was risible; I was far more frightened of them than of a 'grizzled' serial killer called Mad Dog.

Archie's girlfriend (by then, his ex-girlfriend) only got her children back after a week and a promise never to see him again.

Bullying causes feelings of depression, isolation, anxiety and fear. Added to this, a boy Nina was in love with had rejected her, and having internalised the widespread societal message that true love was a one-time event, she believed she was destined to be alone forever.

I found a suicide note in Nina's bedroom: 'This hasn't been an easy decision to make but I've decided that I want to die. My life has been mostly wonderful thanks to you, but due to recent circumstances life has become too painful to live…'

Dr C suggested anti-depressants. She was only fourteen, but our duty first and foremost was to keep her alive, so we agreed. Six years later, my little sister Tricia would take her own life while in a deep depression, and with a diagnosis of bipolar, without leaving a note.

Nina had compelling environmental reasons to be depressed, rather than chemical ones, and is angry to this day that they were not adequately addressed and instead she was put on anti-depressant drugs. I think as her parents, we were so terrified of her dying that we were willing to try anything, and the decision was taken in a blind panic – maybe these pills would help her be happy, *somehow, anyhow.*

Twenty-One

Nina said later that the depression was far more debilitating than the autism: 'At least autism doesn't kill you.'

Having got an autism diagnosis for Nina, I then followed the school doctor's advice and applied for Disability Living Allowance for her. Of all the traumatic experiences in life, filling in a form for your child's disability benefit must come high up on the list. Parents are often advised to describe life at its worst, rather than playing anything down, which is a depressing aim to say the least, and feels insulting to the child in question.

Completing this onerous paperwork for Nina was daunting not only because of the negativity necessary, but also because of the sheer volume of detail required. The thick thirty-page pamphlet of questions required answers with specific examples and timings. The form then had to be backed up with reports and comments from the professionals. To make matters trickier for us, the forms had been designed for children with physical disabilities rather than autism.

Does your child have difficulty walking? Does your child have difficulty washing? Does your child have difficulty coping with their toilet needs? Does your child need medical equipment?

The challenges faced by parents of children with autism are often difficult to describe and difficult to quantify – but quantify them you must. How often? How many times a week? How many times a day? For how many minutes each time?

Some questions appeared to be more relevant but in fact weren't.

Question: Has the child's development of physical and sensory skills been delayed?

Answer: Er...no. The development of her sensory skills

is off the scale – and that's one of the things that causes the problems...

Has the child's development of social skills been delayed? Does the child have difficulty waking, getting up or going to bed? Does your child need someone with them when they are outdoors? Does the child need help with medication?

Does the child need help understanding other people?

Answer: Well, yes... Except the examples on the form included help with lip reading, interpreting sign language...

Is the child unwilling to communicate with other people?

Answer: I am constantly acting as Nina's interpreter to the world. I attract her attention on behalf of other people. I rephrase their questions for them, I interpret her facial expressions and body language when she refuses to give a verbal answer, I try to explain that 'she didn't mean it' when she says something that is interpreted as rude. She often shouts at people, telling them to shut up because she can't stand the noise they are making (it stops her being able to concentrate). She finds the necessary interactions of school life so stressful that she needs to return home for lunch every day...

And the form went on, and relentlessly on...

How often? How many times a week? How many times a day? For how many minutes each time?

If your application is accepted and benefits awarded, these heartbreaking forms must be filled in all over again a year or two down the line, regardless that the child has a lifelong condition.

After the age of sixteen, the child must re-apply themselves – something I could not even bring myself to suggest to Nina when the time came, so the benefits we had only been receiving a few years were quietly shelved.

Twenty-One

A year after her diagnosis, an article appeared in the *Sunday Times* headlined 'SOME "AUTISTIC" CHILDREN AREN'T ILL, THEY'RE JUST BADLY BEHAVED'.

This opinion piece stated that in 1999, there were 114 autistic children in Scotland's secondary schools, and now (2006) there were 825; likewise, in Scottish primary schools, the numbers had risen from 415 to 1,736 in the same period. The journalist, Katie Grant, pronounced that Bill Welsh – the chair of Action Against Autism who had produced this data and who had described it as 'a public health crime' – to be 'well-intentioned' but 'scaremongering in the most sensational way'. 'Look behind these figures,' she said, 'and reports of an epidemic of autism are grossly exaggerated.'

She went on to say that autism had gained a certain 'notoriety' after the MMR inoculation scare (when in 1998 the MMR vaccine was erroneously linked to autism) and then following the publication of Mark Haddon's novel *The Curious Incident of the Dog in the Night-Time* – which had a hero with Asperger's syndrome – it had become 'even more fashionable'.

She went on: 'To the great distress of parents whose children really are on the autistic spectrum, the condition has been adopted by many other parents of children who are not ill, just badly behaved. If a child is described as "autistic", nobody can be angry if he, or more rarely she, throws a tantrum at school or consistently irritates the neighbours.'

Reading this, as a parent of a recently diagnosed autistic child who had had to fight for eight years to get the diagnosis, I was only two columns into the piece, which headed up page three, and I was already shaking with anger. But it got worse: 'Children know that if they suffer from some kind of behaviour "ism" good things result: reduced expectation, indulgence instead of punishment, safety from even the gentlest rebuke.

At the first sign of a teacher's impatience, the child can rush home and cry "abuse". Autism, a serious condition when real, is being exploited by others for all it's worth. And it's worth quite a lot. A diagnosis of some kind of behaviour "ism" might result in £80 a week disability allowance.'

This journalist then went on to criticise my local MSP, who she described as having 'taken it upon herself to brandish the autism statistics about', and who she warned to be careful that she was 'not being taken for a mug'. Ms Grant then went on to demand that we find the 'true reasons' these children are doing badly at school and suggested that 'nine times out of ten' those reasons would be 'family breakdown, community paralysis,' and yes, as sure as night follows day, the inevitable blaming of the parents, or as she phrased it, 'hopeless parenting', which included 'putting a child into a nursery from the age of six weeks where one-to-one communication is minimal'. She confidently declared that 'it is not autism that makes so many children fidget all the time, it is habit'.

This offensive article continued paragraph after nauseating paragraph, as hideous to read today as it was then. 'Children unused to staring at anything static or making conversation that does not consist of grunts are bound to appear strange.'

As I re-read it, almost every sentence is worthy of repeating here for its sheer ignorance and arrogance, even if I do have the urge to handle each one wearing a hazmat suit and rubber gloves.

But she was not finished. Her final paragraph began: 'There are no perfect parents. But it must surely be the worst kind of damage to label your child with an "ism" when there is nothing wrong except that you've not done a great job at child rearing.'

I remember the morning I first read this piece being incandescent with rage – beside myself with fury (every cliché works) and unable to focus on anything else. Cello worked for the

Twenty-One

Sunday Times at the time and phoned the news editor to tell him about my distress. The news editor suggested I write to Katie Grant and express my anger and he would pass it on to her.

So I did.

Dear Katie Grant,

Your article is so ill-informed that it's difficult to know how to begin to introduce you to the world of autism. But here goes.

Doctors do not diagnose autism lightly. My daughter was diagnosed last year at the age of ten. The diagnosis was made after an intensive six-month assessment period in which class teachers, a speech and language therapist, an educational psychologist, the school paediatrician and three psychiatrists were consulted. Doctors bend over backwards not to 'label' a child.

No child wants to be different. To suggest that children want to be diagnosed with a disability because 'good things result' is breathtakingly insensitive. My daughter is desperate to be like everyone else. Difficulties arise daily because of her condition, yet she hasn't summoned up the courage to confide in her friends about her diagnosis, let alone rushed home crying 'abuse'.

To fill out a form for Disability Living Allowance for one of your children is one of the saddest things a parent will ever do. Believe me, I know: I've done it and I cried throughout the several hours it took to complete it. Have you seen the criteria that have to be fulfilled? You should take a look. It may make you realise how much you have been smugly taking for granted with your own children.

Thank goodness there are people in the public eye like Christine Graham MSP, who is fighting for more help for people with autism. We need people like her to help undo the damage ignorant articles like yours cause. You argue that once a child is diagnosed, they get away with bad behaviour. In fact, very few allowances are made and very little credit given for the enormous effort it takes my daughter to fit in (to the extent that she can). Articles like yours impede the public's understanding and make life even harder for her.

No parent asks for their child to be given a diagnosis for a life-long disability lightly. On the contrary, I'm sure that there are lots of undiagnosed children out there because parents find it too difficult to face the fact that their child may have autism. For you to imply that we are chasing a diagnosis because it is fashionable, or an easy get-out, defies belief. I'm sure that many families feel the same. These are the same families that you just kicked when they were down.

Inevitably, you blame 'hopeless parenting'… Ironically, parents of autistic children are usually the most skilled parents there are – because they have to deal with situations other parents never even dream of.

You refer to children 'unused to staring at anything static'. In fact, my daughter is a voracious reader. Thank goodness she did not happen to read your Sunday Times piece. What would that have done to her self-esteem? Did the thought that you may be hurting some very vulnerable people enter your head when you wrote this article?

I have another daughter who does not have autism. Raising her to be happy and considerate and fulfilled is a walk in the park in comparison to raising a child with autism. Luckily, I have my daughter with autism to teach me some humility and stop me from becoming insufferably smug, a trap you have demonstrated is very easy to fall into.

Cello emailed my letter over to the *Sunday Times* Scotland news desk.

I had never been on Mumsnet then, but looking back now I see this article triggered a stream of furious comments.

'KG appears to have about as much understanding about autism as my cat.'

'This ignorance spreads and increases the tut tut chorus.'

'Idiots like this make my life one hundred times harder.'

Twenty-One

'I want to ram this article down this smug woman's throat.'
'I feel like crying after reading that.'
'I read that and my eyes went hot.'
They were still responding months later:
'HOW FUCKING DARE SHE.'

Within a few days, I received a reply in which the journalist apologised for causing 'such pain and distress'. She explained that she had been trying to question the huge rise in numbers rather than argue autism did not exist. 'But I can see that whether my intentions were good or not, the result was very unhappy.' She acknowledged that she had hurt people and her language had offended, and she seemed genuinely sorry. 'This is a topic that should have been approached with more caution and your criticisms about smugness are well taken.'

Trouble erupted at school so often that I felt nervous about leaving the house or being out of contact or too far away. One solution was for me to begin some home study. My Uncle Gerald had recently died and left me a small legacy, so when a friend told me she was starting a creative writing course with the Open University, I found myself saying, 'So am I.'

This seemed the perfect use for money left by my uncle – a man born with a hip disability that curtailed his life and his freedom and who had left school at fourteen. Being a writer had been a dream since I was a child, but a dream I had allowed to be pushed aside by 'real life' until it had almost disappeared from view. The fear of failing that had always lurked at the back of my mind had been replaced with the fear of never beginning. Being tied to the house created the perfect opportunity to put this dream to the test see if I could indeed write.

Twenty-Two

I started looking into home schooling but knew that at secondary level, I could not do justice to Nina's intelligence and capabilities. I didn't even have an O Level in a foreign language, let alone a Scottish Higher in one. I hated maths and I'd bluffed my way through the sciences.

The school denied that Nina was being picked on or victimised, 'because,' said the deputy head, 'all pupils are taught in PSE (Personal Social Education) to respect all differences between people.'

The gulf, the great gulf, no, the *y a w n i n g* chasm between theory and practice, right there.

Nina had been given permission to go to the Special Needs Base if she needed somewhere safe at school. She had recently been outed as bisexual and during one art lesson, a group of girls began loudly discussing this, including one girl I used to give shelter to at our house when her dad was in the pub. The teacher did not intervene in the bullying, so after the class, Nina set off as fast as she could towards the Special Needs Base. The girls caught up with her. One of them kicked her from behind and knocked her down the stairs, then the others joined in.

Because this was physical bullying with physical marks, the school could not ignore it. The ringleader did not even deny it. Her father was brought in, the headteacher wagged his finger at her and told her never to do it again. She was not suspended, not even for a day. The other girls weren't even confronted with what they had done. Quite how the school thought they were teaching pupils to 'respect differences between people' by acting in this way, I do not know.

Twenty-Two

If we consider how an adult would be dealt with if they kicked a colleague in the workplace down the stairs, it highlights how grossly inadequate this response was, and how inadequately we protect children.

Inevitably, in the circumstances, the bullying did not stop.

I felt isolated and terrified, so I can only imagine how Nina felt.

The headteacher, it seemed, put more emphasis on wearing the right school uniform than on not bullying other pupils. Correct uniform was the be-all and end-all – kids were sent home if they wore black trainers rather than black shoes, but they apparently weren't sent home if they kicked another pupil down the stairs.

This was despite the school claiming to have a 'zero tolerance policy' approach to bullying; a zero tolerance approach that was easy to say but meant nothing.

'We grow accustomed to the dark,' said Emily Dickinson, but when 'the dark' is your child being bullied, we do not become accustomed to it. We *never* become accustomed to it because this dark is a fresh hellish dark each time.

I bear a grudge.

I do not forgive the people who bullied Nina; indeed, my anger still flashes like a solar flare. I know this is not what I am supposed to say. I know they were children. I know the perceived wisdom is that the only person I am hurting by not forgiving is myself; that to be unforgiving is to poison myself. But nevertheless, I have not forgiven, and I have no wish to do so. The children who mocked, ostracised and assaulted Nina never made any attempt to apologise or showed any remorse. They never received any punishment. The bullying did not stop until we physically took Nina out of harm's way. I believe that at least one of them was a victim of a neglectful upbringing, but still, I do not forgive.

I could go so far as to say that, like *Tam O Shanter's* Kate, I do not want to 'make peace with what I cannot change' and, Kate-style, I am still 'nursing my wrath to keep it warm'. I am not in need of any of the release promised to a forgiver.

Is it that I can't forgive, or that I won't? Is it somehow compulsive or enjoyable not to forgive? Is it a version of prodding a sore tooth? I do not consider myself a vengeful or a vindictive person. I can forgive people who have hurt me – and indeed rarely take things personally – but I now know that I cannot forgive people who have hurt my children. And maybe it is not up to me to forgive them anyway, maybe only Nina can do that.

But for those who were kind to Nina, I will always be grateful. For the children and teachers who showed empathy; for instance, the maths teacher who, on the first day at high school, asked Nina a question and when she got it right threw her a Penguin biscuit right across the classroom as a reward. For those people, I am eternally grateful.

There is no middle ground with this, only emotions at the extremes.

A day or two after her attacker was not suspended, Nina phoned from school, having been bullied yet again, and said, 'Please, just buy me some books and let me stay at home. *Please.*'

And there it was, the straw that broke the camel's back. A moment of release, of letting go of the belief that I had somehow to *make* Nina fit in in this way. This could not go on.

'Yes,' I said, 'we'll find another way.'

It was such a relief to finally decide that enough was enough and somehow or other we would remove her from a

Twenty-Two

place in which I didn't think she had ever felt safe.

The school's motto was PRIDE, standing for Participation, Respect, Inclusion, Determination and Excellence. American activist Verna Myers said, 'Diversity is being invited to the party; inclusion is being asked to dance.' Nina was never metaphorically or literally asked to dance at that school, let alone being made to feel accepted enough *to ask someone else to dance*. Oh, except once when she did ask a boy to dance in a Scottish country dancing lesson at primary school and he rolled his eyes in disgust.

There's 'inclusion', then there's *inclusion*.

A report from the University of Wisconsin-Madison in 2009 said that mothers of children with autism had chronic stress levels comparable to combat soldiers. I can believe it. But if that is the case, what are the stress levels of the autistic children themselves?

We went to meet the staff at the Edinburgh Steiner School. Nina and Lara had taken part in a fortnight's summer school there several times as young primary pupils and had loved it, so I was familiar with the big gardens, the rope swings dangling from the trees, the home baking, the love of music making and storytelling.

It took a few days for Nina to meet the staff and to be accepted as a pupil and so I suggested that she tell no one at the local high school until her new place was finalised, but it must have been too big a relief for her to keep it to herself.

'Er, Nina says she's leaving…' said the deputy head over the phone the following day.

'Yep,' I said, and it was all I could do not to add, 'Too right she's leaving, you bunch of bastards.'

Nina settled immediately into the Steiner School. No matter that we had a twenty-mile round trip morning and evening. No matter we had to pay for her education (although it was a stretch for us, and I was aware that this option would not be open to everyone). No matter that once again, it was Nina who had to change, not the bullies. The important thing was that having left the local high school, she was immediately happier, and that happiness rubbed off on the rest of the family.

For a short time, I had been free of the dreaded school run; once Lara had started walking herself to school, I had thought that part of my life was over. Now here I was driving much further, this time from our commuter town into central Edinburgh and back, every day, twice a day. Nina found listening to Radio 4 stressful because 'It's always about some rapist, and I already know that a lot of people are shit,' so we played CDs of her choice. For the whole first term, it was *Lungs* by Florence and the Machine, on repeat, keeping us company as we drove out through the woods and farmland before joining the inner-city traffic jams – on some memorable mornings that first winter in temperatures as low as minus ten degrees – to reach the blessed sanctuary of this new school. 'The dog days are over,' sang Florence Welsh, over and over, 'The dog days are over,' and we dared to hope that now Nina was fourteen and in a safe place that our dog days – days of bad luck and unrest, according to the ancient Romans – may indeed be over.

On the journey home, I would play a CD of Homer's epic poem *The Odyssey*, which was a gift from Cello and seemed appropriate as it told the story of Odysseus's journey home after a ten-year war and all the perils he had to overcome – not school bullies, ill-informed medics or hostile headmasters, but the cyclops, the sirens, sea monsters and the lotus-eaters – to reach a place of safety.

Twenty-Two

At Steiners, Nina was amazed to find people 'being themselves' and all dressing differently to express who they were, because there was no rigid school uniform policy here. The only hitch came when she was asked not to wear T-shirts with images of skulls dripping blood on the front, because she was 'frightening the kindergarten'. She stopped wearing the offending T-shirts but disputed the situation: 'Actually, it's a rotting vampire called Miss Deadbeat, and anyway,' she added, 'the kindergarteners aren't scared of me, they think I'm cool.' In fact, she did a little research and asked the kindergarteners what they were really frightened of, to which they replied: 'thunderstorms and wolves'.

At about this time, I cleared out the dressing up box at home with its green Tinkerbell costume, its blue Cinderella ballgown and selection of spangled tutus, all bought from the Disney Store on Princes Street and loved by Nina and Lara when they were younger. I phoned Steiners and offered these little costumes to the kindergarten for dressing up, but encountered a very sceptical response: 'Oh, I don't think we'd want *those*.' And I felt I'd tried to off-load a bag of nuclear waste.

I should have known better because when we had toured the school, I noticed that the children in the kindergarten were playing with a pile of stones, dried leaves and sticks in a wicker handmade basket.

I dropped Nina off one day and watched another pupil shoot through the school gate riding a unicycle, presumably in readiness for the circus skills course, and two more children in hand-knitted jumpers arriving in a cart pulled by a bike.

There was an odd juxtaposition on that wide, tree-lined road in suburban Edinburgh because opposite the school, with its cast of brightly coloured individuals, was a centre for the Mormon Church. So, on the opposite pavement to the pupils ready for circus skills, I'd see young male missionaries with their startling teeth, identical super-short haircuts, suits and smiles, apparent identikits, setting off for the day's evangelising. Occasionally, I'd also see the female missionaries, walking in pairs, wearing their ankle-skimming dresses and identical long straight hair. I have read that the dress and grooming code for the Mormon missionaries is intended to be 'nothing that detracts from the spirit or draws undue attention for being extreme,' but to me their cookie cutter look was more remarkable and attention-grabbing than the multi-coloured Steiner individuality or even Nina's Miss Deadbeat T-shirt.

Nina had her hair cut into a mohawk but would have to wait until she was eighteen and had eventually left the school to dye it red because she had pushed the no uniform rule to its limits.

At this school, there were no self-assessment worksheets on *Do you Attract New Friends Easily?* or *How Interesting are You?* Here, there were lessons in juggling and Aristotle, productions of plays by the ancient Greeks, lessons in map making and archaeology, sculpting, comedy and tragedy. Two-hour morning lessons for the sake of learning widely, with no exam at the end: lessons for the pure joy of finding out, discovering and exploring the world beyond the national curriculum.

There was an ethos of kindness and acceptance at the school, and less emphasis on conforming that allowed Nina to dare to tell her classmates about her autism. She called it 'coming out' because she was making herself vulnerable and disclosing a fundamental part of her identity.

She reported back: 'No one called me a "retard"!', a word she found highly offensive and that had been thrown around, including at her personally, at her previous school. Her new classmates were interested in her autism and then they accepted it. In fact, her friend Anna said, 'Oh, I know, you're autistic. I noticed that on the first day.'

Twenty-Two

The school run brought with it an unexpected bonus. Twice a day, I passed Napier University, which ran an MA course in creative writing, and as I drove past this establishment's front gates, I caught tantalising glimpses of the ivory towers within. I could feel fate drumming its fingers, muttering impatiently, 'Well? Come on, then…What are you waiting for?'

I had just completed two years studying creative writing with the Open University, but knew there was more I wanted to learn. Plus, there was what appeared to be an impossibly closed literary world that I wanted to break into. I knew no published writers and barely any amateur writers. Maybe this was my way in.

Upon discovering at the MA interview that the creative writing course had what they referred to as a Writers' Room – a room lined with books, with views over the lawns, comfy sofas on which to read, desks at which to write, and where other would-be writers congregated to chat – this course felt like a gift from the gods.

The 'ivory towers' I had glimpsed while on the school run were in fact built as a Victorian asylum to resemble a luxury country house because it was believed that the well-off, fee-paying, mentally ill clientele would benefit from 'bright and pleasant' surroundings. By the time fate led me to these grade A listed buildings, they had been part of the university for twenty years.

I began the part-time MA in Creative Writing the following September, which fitted in perfectly with Nina's school run. I was one of the oldest, but no matter, I threw myself in with gratitude and high excitement.

The course was mind-bending and eye-opening. I read authors I had never heard of. I read genres I hadn't known existed. *'Graphic' novels? What are they? Sex and violence?* I grappled with philosophers whose names I had never spoken out loud and whose ephemeral literary theories glittered bright and fascinating one moment before slipping through my fingers again the next. I revelled in the course; the three-act structure, the five-act structure, discussions about point of view, writing in first person, writing in third person.

I loved it all – even the stuff the lecturers had surely made up. *The Oulipo?* 'So, you're saying this chap Perec wrote a 300-page book without using the letter e. But, but…why? Is this a joke?'

'Er, no,' replied the lecturer, peering hard over her spectacles, a little affronted.

My classmate, Anne – the only other one of a similar age to me – and I made wide eyes at each other and stifled a laugh. Some people really knew how to make life hard, eh?

How I loved this strange and wonderful world of literature where apparently nobody batted an eyelid if you decided to write an entire book without the letter e.

I told a childfree friend that I wanted to write a book about motherhood and what it was *really* like. 'Oh, there are lots of those,' she replied. And I thought, *Are there?* How had I missed them? Had I been purposefully blind? But even if there were, were they real? Did they tell it as it truly was? Motherhood: a tragicomedy.

One day on the creative writing course, we were set a writing exercise. I don't remember what the exercise was, but I wrote about a woman peeling potatoes at the kitchen sink who was so miserable that she began to disappear from her finger ends up. Then I asked myself, why wouldn't this character just leave this situation? I decided she was married and lived on an isolated farm – but still, I wondered, why would she not leave if she was so miserable? I could picture her child sitting at the

Twenty-Two

kitchen table behind her – but, surely, she could take the child with her if she left? Then I thought, but what if the child was autistic and frightened of the world? What if the child could not leave, and therefore she could not leave without him?

I began to write a novel called *Truestory* about characters living through this scenario for my MA's final project. Rather than making the autistic child a girl though, I made them a boy to distance the real Nina from this fictional story. It was therapeutic to have my characters struggle with many of the situations my real life family had faced over the previous years.

After graduating from the Creative Writing course, I continued work on *Truestory* at home rather than in the writers' room. By then, the beautiful buildings – the ivory towers – were being sold off and converted into luxury apartments. But for me, during the two years of the course, those buildings had indeed been a bright, pleasant and perfect refuge.

Now I was writing at a computer, which was placed on a long desk between my daughters' computers in their playroom. My keyboard had been put in such a central position after a nine-year-old friend of Nina's visited and I discovered Google searches including 'laddies with no cloths on'.

As I sat at my computer trying to write my 1000 words a day, to my right-hand side was Lara playing online games on the Club Penguin site where her penguin character called Kebo (named after our cat) could build an igloo and decorate it, and to my left was Nina playing *The Sims* in which she created online families and communities and managed her characters' moods and health, but freaked out when things went wrong and the black-hooded figure of the grim reaper materialised to collect them.

In my novel, the autistic character was a twelve-year-old

boy called Sam, and when I wanted inspiration for how Sam might react in a certain situation, I looked to my left and consulted Nina to see what she thought.

'Nina, what skills have you learned online?'

'Nina, what kind of things do you think of as lucky?'

I gave Sam fears of unwrapped presents and plug holes and nettles (which Nina had had as a child), but also gave him a terror of the colour yellow, a fear of eating more than nineteen pieces of pasta on one plate, and an inability to travel more than 823 steps from his home (which Nina hadn't).

I also created a host of characters who met up online to post messages in a chatroom and discuss things like 'How do I know what to believe?' and 'Do wishes come true?' One of these chatroom characters was inspired by the contemporary teenaged Nina. This character was a very rational, opinionated, feisty, straight-talking, intelligent girl called Fizzy Mascara (an online name Nina had used herself at times), and when I wanted to know what this character thought, I would lean over to my left and consult Nina again.

So, although *Truestory* was a work of fiction, Nina appeared in it twice – once as a twelve-year-old autistic boy and again as the radical outspoken young woman she had become.

The main character in *Truestory*, the mother, Alice, decides to 'jump off the world' along with her son; to live a small life, a life cut off from the rest of the world, away from the difficulties of trying to fit an autistic child into a non-autistic world – something I had often imagined doing myself, but which I could never have actually done because I had two children with different needs to care for.

On one of those twenty-mile round trips to school, I commented to fifteen-year-old Nina, 'I wish I had a brain like

Twenty-Two

yours.' She looked disbelieving. 'What are you on about?' I pointed out how intelligent she was, how she had started reading at eighteen months and could recite the alphabet at two; how she could read a fact and remember it for years; how she could read an entire book in a day and recall it all. I told her I knew that she hated her autism, but it was the autism that helped her to process information in an amazing way.

She told me later that something clicked in her brain that day; that until then she had longed for a 'cure'. She hadn't realised that her brain was unusual in this way – she thought everyone could do what she could do. She said it hurt to know that not everyone could store and access huge amounts of information like she could, because these abilities made her even more different than ever, but it also helped her to realise there were good aspects to her diagnosis – and she became grateful for them. She no longer hoped for a cure because she appreciated her talents and did not want to lose them.

She wrote a piece about this for the national Steiner magazine, *New View*, under the headline 'LIVING WITH ASPERGER'S SYNDROME – AN ESSAY'. This was the first time she had gone public to a wider audience about her autism.

She described how she had wandered her old school playgrounds by herself, daydreaming and eating. She said she believed it was her fate to be unpopular, adding: 'The older I grew, the worse I felt about this. While other girls were forming groups of close friends and learning dance routines and giggling together, I watched from the sidelines wondering what they had that I didn't. I was asking myself the wrong question: I should have been wondering what I had that they didn't, and in Primary Five, I finally found out.'

She went on to describe how being different got more and more distressing until when she was in Primary Seven, she had begun to self-harm by biting herself.

'I really savaged myself. Sometimes people would ask me what the purple marks on my arms were, but I'd just pretend not to hear them.'

She wrote of how things got even worse on starting high school, with the increased pressure to fit in and conform. She described how she formulated a plan and vowed to 'become exactly like the other girls. I would wear clothes like theirs. I would become normal, and maybe I would even become popular.'

But her plan was doomed to fail because 'Although I now looked like the scary girls, I didn't act, speak or think like them.' She continued to be interested in politics and current affairs rather than boys and clothes, so, 'Even after making my mum spend a fortune on new make-up, clothes and hair products, I was no more popular than before. Not only that, I had hidden who I really was, shielding myself behind a mask of make-up.'

She described her impression of her new school: 'I knew the ethos at Steiners was completely different.' Instead of everyone being the same, 'the place was a rainbow of different colours and styles, and people who weren't afraid to be themselves. This threw my idea of what "normal" was and I had to accept that there is no such thing.'

When her piece was published, she received a standard letter from the editor with a hand-written addendum: 'I thought what you wrote was a very fine and honest piece.'

Although I was forty-five and I was the one attending a creative writing course, Nina at the age of fifteen had beaten me to it in getting a personal piece published in a magazine, and I couldn't have been happier.

Twenty-Two

Despite all the difficulties in those early years, I had an urge to hold onto Nina and Lara's childhoods. When they were in their teens, I dragged a plastic tub of baby clothes out of the attic. In it were tiny cotton dresses from babyhood – some as wide as they were long to fit over nappies – and I turned them into two memory quilts, one for each of them.

'How can you cut them up?' Shuddered another mother. 'I could *never* do that.'

I cut a five-inch template out of a cornflake packet and, taking each dress in turn, I cut off the complicated bits, the collars and cuffs, the gathers, the pockets, the buttons and the hems, and I used the template to cut a pile of perfect squares.

Some dresses were only big enough to make two squares – one from the front and one from the back. Each patchwork square was a different colour and design, and held different memories and stories. They were tactile mementoes. Many were gifts; there were impractical dresses with lacy collars that had flipped up and got coated in baby food, dresses with tight puffed sleeves that were impossible to thread a fat baby's arm through. There were pinafores, sun dresses, and any number of party dresses, in green gingham, blue ticking, pink jersey and every floral under the sun.

I cut a cerise flowery square from the dress Nina wore on a day trip to Fleetwood, a mustard paisley square from the dungarees Lara wore to Elizabeth's wedding, a square of yellow irises from Nina's dress for Hilary's wedding.

When I see the quilts now, in all their riotous joyful chaos on the girls' beds, I think about the shuddering mother and her bags of out-of-fashion baby clothes still festering in her attic.

I also rooted in my own attic and found bags of the children's old jumpers and fleeces and turned those into hundreds

Hold Fast

of strips that I wove into hessian to make rag rugs. Again, each colour and rag strip brought back memories of dimpled faces, cuddles, smiles and fat limbs, and in that jewel-bright jumbled context, all the memories were good.

However, when I attended a writing workshop for performance poetry a few years later, I was asked to 'write for ten minutes on something you feel very strongly about' and I didn't even hesitate: 'Thank God you're grown', I wrote, my pen flying over the page:

Thank God You're Grown
No more Brownies, Rainbows, Guides,
Tiny Tumbles, Tumble Tots, Tiny Teds
No more Ju-jitsu, karate, football skillz for girlz.

Thank God you're grown
No more classmates on playdates
'Would little Bryony/Natalie/Chelsea come for tea?'
What does she eat?
Oh, only chips and nuggets and jello if it's yellow
with sprinkles pink and sweet enough to break your teeth.

Thank God you're grown.
No more school concerts, Sports days, nativity plays
An encore? Please, God, no.
They grow up too quick, they love to say,

But not for me.
No more Nats and mocks, NABs and NARs,
No more Duke of Edinburgh Awards

Twenty-Two

Every day, I'm glad you're grown
And here to stop me getting old.
From lessons on Instagram, Twitter and emojis,
Facetime, memes and the perfect selfies.
With words for things we never described: cis, transgender, non-binary,
You update me with tighter trousers, shorter socks,
Bought not at Tesco but at Top Shop.

You teach me class tunes by Bruno Mars
How to join in Carpool Karaoke
How to mix a French Martini
How to Keep up with a Kardashian
How to enjoy the wisdom of Will-i-am

But best of all you teach me to swear:
You chattin shit? Fuck me running!
I'm glad you're grown and here right now
To stop me fossilising
with your acronyms,
I'm LOLing & ROFLing,
Cos being your mum is Pure. Bang. Tidy.

A poem that, after it was published in an Edinburgh Literary Salon anthology *Lost Looking & Found*, whenever I performed it at events and open mics, made other mothers my age come to me and say, with a shake of the head and a look of painful recognition, 'Oh, Nats and mocks…Oh God, Duke of Edinburgh Awards…Oh, that poem…'

Twenty-Three

Nina continued her love affair with learning and, as she is bisexual, took a special interest in women's rights and the LGBT+ community. She loved to discuss these issues whenever possible which, when considering her unfiltered communication style, created some interesting situations.

One day, Nina, Lara and I were at a Scottish spa hotel sitting in the jacuzzi when we realised the lady beside us was American. Nina asked where she was from and was told South Carolina. This was several years before the overturning of Roe v Wade, so the subject of abortion was not often openly discussed, but Nina had sensed the way the wind was blowing in the USA. 'Oh, it can be difficult to get an abortion in South Carolina,' she said, conversationally, 'How do you cope? Do you use double contraceptives?'

There followed one of those moments where everything stills, including the lady from South Carolina, and the silence becomes deafening. Maybe the jacuzzi even stopped bubbling. I caught Lara's eye as she sank back into an alcove, like the meme of Homer Simpson sinking into a hedge. We left shortly after.

On another occasion, we were sharing a table at a banquet in a Mexican resort, and when we told the Yorkshire couple beside us that we were from Scotland they replied, 'We're from the UK.' We asked them about their plans for the holiday and they told us that, no, they would not be travelling the one hundred miles from the resort to see Chichen Itza – one of the seven wonders of the modern world – because their son had already visited it and had shown them his photos on Facebook. They told us a lot about this dearly beloved

Twenty-Three

son, their literal golden-haired, blue-eyed boy, and they took out their phones to scroll through their many photos of him, passing them around. 'He's very successful at work,' said Mrs UK. 'He doesn't have time for a girlfriend,' added Mr UK, to which Nina, without looking up from her chicken topped with teriyaki foam, replied, with no judgement, just stating a fact: 'Perhaps he's asexual.'

After Nina turned seventeen, the school run took on a new purpose – driving practice. This fell to me, despite me being the most nervous of passengers, so I would drive Nina to school in the morning and she would drive us back in the afternoon. She was keen to learn and to get her driving licence, so I was keen to help – although in truth, I would rather have done almost anything than take part in this white-knuckle ride.

One day as we headed home along the country road outside Edinburgh, Nina mistakenly got stuck in neutral while trying to change from fourth gear to fifth and haphazardly tried to pull over, driving off the road onto the very bumpy grass verge with a ditch down the other side – which we fortunately just missed. A stream of cars behind waited as Nina got the engine restarted and went through the mirror signal manoeuvre routine – not one toot, not one angry honk did they make, and I still remember, with much gratitude, their kindness to this learner driver. This incident did not put Nina off and she soon passed her test – another achievement that I had never taken for granted.

When Nina reached the age of eighteen, she should officially have been discharged by Dr C who was based at CAMHS, the Child and Adolescent Mental Health Services. Nina was still seeing Dr C regularly at that point so the doctor could assess

Nina's use of melatonin and anti-depressants, and it felt reassuring to have access to her expertise. Dr C suggested she keep Nina on her books for an additional year, I think out of kindness, but the day eventually came when Nina was nineteen and the discharge became inevitable, and we had to say goodbye.

This was terrifying: it meant having no named person to contact if a crisis occurred, and it felt like we had been thrust naked out of the igloo.

It also left a teenager on anti-depressants with no information about how to ever come off them.

The first time a crisis *did* occur, and we needed support, we had to go to the GP who consulted someone by phone at the psychiatric hospital and then relayed a message back to us. It was help at arm's length from a faceless medic from behind the walls of the Royal Edinburgh Psychiatric Hospital and, after fighting for years to get help for Nina, we knew we were back out in the cold.

When Nina was eighteen, I published my novel, *Truestory*, which was set on a farm similar to the one on which I had been brought up. *The Herald* newspaper, in an interview with me, described it as 'most definitely not an everyday story of countryfolk'. I had met the *Herald* journalist at the Scots Club in Edinburgh to discuss the book shortly before publication. She was a stylish woman, wearing big jewellery, and as we sat in this New Town club, all tartan and polished dark wood and rustling newspapers, I felt surreally as though I was poking my head into an adult world after years of motherhood and studenthood; an adult parallel universe that had apparently been there all along full of adults, doing adult things.

Even though the novel was about a mother bringing up a child with autism, it had never crossed my mind to write

Twenty-Three

a memoir. I wouldn't have dared; it would have felt far too exposing for myself and too intrusive for Nina. Despite me making the character with autism a boy to try to create some distance from Nina, when the book came out, Lara read it and said, 'Well, it might be fiction, but Nina is on every page of this book.'

I described *Truestory* as being 'inspired' by my experiences of raising a child with autism, rather than 'based on', but I could tell some readers were sceptical. Some seemed to assume it was all based on truth (after all, it *was* confusingly called *Truestory*).

'I have never had sex in a polytunnel!' I would point out, alluding to an event in the book. 'I have not had an affair with an itinerant worker!'

But still, people were not convinced. More than once, I was asked, *What does your husband think about you writing about him like that?* And I would try again to explain that my knowledge of raising an autistic child was garnered from real life but the characters and events in the book were purely fictional. 'Yes,' they would insist, looking sidelong, 'but what does he *really* think?'

'Is it terrible having a writer in the family?' I asked Nina, recalling the old adage that having a writer in the family was as bad as having a murderer, and Nina replied, 'Why? I can always write back.'

The book was launched at Waterstones on Princes Street, with the huge second-floor windows framing a view of the castle – the same view I had had from the car window that first time I stumbled into the city more than twenty years earlier on my first visit to Cello. The same Waterstones where I had spent all those Sunday afternoons several years after that first visit, hiding at the back of the store with my face to the shelves, trying to absorb information about invisible disabilities.

Hold Fast

What a long and convoluted journey, what an odyssey, I had been on, from hiding at the back of the shop to reading out loud from my own book at the front; from being a terrified and confused first-time mother to being a better-informed mother of two.

At the time of publication, I had never heard the term 'Autism Mom' and maybe I would never have written the novel if I had for fear of being labelled one. Autism Mom is a phrase used by the autistic community to describe the mothers of autistic children who use this as their identity, mothers who talk of their children as burdensome and tragic, and – as Nina puts it – as though their autistic children are 'dead behind the eyes'. Autism Moms are seen as mothers who imply that their autistic children have ruined their lives, that their lives are full of the tragedy of autism, that they are martyrs to their child's autism and that their only hope lies in finding a cure.

I do not identify with this group, but it is true that raising Nina has had a profound effect on me and my life, mainly teaching me how determined I can be.

Nina and I used my novel to campaign for autism awareness, and later, when that no longer seemed enough, for autism acceptance. Eventually, Nina would begin to use the phrases 'autism liberation' and 'autism pride'.

Nina said *Truestory* was helpful because it showed an autistic character who was sympathetic, and it demonstrated that 'we can't turn our weird off'. We went on Radio 4's *The Listening Project* to talk about the experience of her receiving her diagnosis, and were featured in the press with headlines like 'THE GIRL WHO IS PROUD TO BE AUTISTIC' and 'AUTISM MADE MY GIRL'S LIFE HARD. BULLIES MADE IT HELL.'

Twenty-Three

Nina's Higher results (the Scottish equivalent of A Levels) were due on the day the four of us arrived back in the country after a family holiday in Cuba. As we waited for our cases, Nina's phone pinged informing her that the results were in. I braced myself. She looked much cooler than I felt and scrolled though her phone. She had achieved four A* grades, which meant she had secured a place at Edinburgh University. These results gave me a physical jolt, and by Heathrow's luggage carousel, I sat down and wept.

I cried out of sheer exhilarated relief that despite all the miseries of the pre-Steiner schooling, Nina had emerged triumphant. She had survived the secondary school experience and had now grown beyond the obligations of being a child in our education system – the obligation to be obedient come what may, to be compliant for compliance's sake, to not 'talk back' no matter how unfair the situation in which you find yourself. A child defending themselves to an authority figure can be termed 'backchat', whereas it would be admirable assertiveness from an adult. We expect children to cope with being treated in ways we would never treat an adult. We set them higher standards than we do adults.

To this day, even though both of my daughters are now adults, I still thank my lucky stars that we are all free of the education system.

When Nina was twenty-one, The Institute for Advanced Studies in the Humanities (IASH) at Edinburgh University asked for written submissions – poems, essays, stories – on the subject of 'What is a Dangerous Women', and having seen Nina fearlessly ask and answer questions about autism, I sent them this:

My Daughter is a Dangerous Woman

My daughter is a dangerous woman because she is autistic and proud of it.
My daughter is a dangerous woman because she asks questions like:
- *Who are you to tell me the way I think is wrong?*
- *Who are you to look down on me?*
- *Who are you to leave me out and think I won't notice?*
- *Who are you to make decisions about autism without asking for an autistic opinion?*
- *Who are you to label me disordered?*
- *Who are you to tell me I'm inspiring while pitying me?*
- *Who are you to tell me what will make me happy?*
- *Who are you to tell me to be normal?*
- *Who are you to tell me how to live?*

Each line of the piece was illustrated by a different selfie taken by Nina over the previous four years. For a long time, her camera had been filled with endless selfies as she experimented with her identity. There were pictures of her with a shorn head, purple eyeshadow and chandelier earrings; with pink hair, black lipstick and a nose ring; with a long purple wig; with a black mohawk and a T-shirt reading 'Punk is Dead'; with a red mohawk; with an elfin cut and a pierced eyebrow. Nina's identity had been a work of art in progress for years by this point. Sometime later, her photograph was spotted by a friend on a street fashion website; a view of her from the back as she strode down the pavement wearing multi-coloured trousers, a self-customised denim cut off, a rainbow bag and a red mohawk. 'What a vibe!' read the caption.

The *My Daughter is a Dangerous Woman* photo-poem was selected to be included in the project, so Nina took her place in a gallery of other Dangerous Women: sculptors, scientists,

Twenty-Three

feminists, eccentrics, thinkers and campaigners – all women who dared to think differently, who dared to *be* different.

We discovered that Nina had a real talent for talking about her autism in an engaging and accessible way. She was articulate and funny in front of an audience, totally unfazed by talking to a sea of faces in a way she often was not when speaking one-on-one. She explained this was because 'If you have an audience, you're in the position of authority, even if the audience is small. Speaking one-on-one is more likely to expose you to impoliteness or hostility.'

She would start right at the beginning, in what she referred to as Autism 101:

Autism is a neurotype (type of brain) which is divergent from the medical 'norm'. It's estimated that around 2 per cent of people are autistic, but the estimate continues to climb due to increasing awareness and a resulting increase in diagnoses. A person who is not autistic is allistic, and a person whose brain entirely corresponds with the medical 'norm' is neurotypical. Autism is present from birth and appears to be genetic…

When, at one of the talks, another autistic person questioned whether it was right to be 'proud' of being autistic, as autism was not something that had been worked for and just *was*, Nina responded by saying, 'All right, maybe the word is *unashamed*.' She explained that for her, embracing her diagnosis had been empowering, that she believed it should be neither taboo nor embarrassing, and that although she may experience the world differently from a neurotypical person, that was neither a weakness nor a failing. She went on to say that if she did not believe in herself nor accept herself, it was going to be an uphill struggle to get anyone else or society in general to accept her and celebrate her.

At one event, a young man strode up to her, smiling broadly after our talk, holding out his hand to shake hands with Nina, and said, 'You are the Martin Luther King of the autism world!' I heard Nina laugh and I'm sure she was proud – but not as proud as me.

Nina went on to study German at Edinburgh University, having never spoken a word of it until she started at Steiners. I could see the faces of the other parents at the autism acceptance events we did, and the looks of intense hope when they heard how Nina had turned her life around, had escaped the bullies by leaving a school she hated, had made friends, had achieved the results, and survived to what I referred to as our 'happy ending'.

For her third year at university, it was necessary for Nina to spend several months in Germany. This prospect had been so frightening when she began her course that I had initially turned my thoughts away from it. However, when the time came, we helped Nina pack her bags and we delivered her to Edinburgh Airport where she excitedly waved us goodbye, grinning for photographs as she held her passport aloft before striding off through the departure gate with barely a backward glance. She had chosen to go to the Baltic coast in Schleswig-Holstein – wanting somewhere she would be forced to speak German. It was somewhere that felt very far away from us – 1,000 miles away to be precise, a four-hour flight to the nearest big city of Hamburg, a seventeen-and-a-half-hour drive, a two-hundred-hour walk.

She started work as a language assistant in a secondary school in Wendorf and through contacts she met Katrin, a widow with a large house, an empty bedroom, a motherly nature, and a desire for a lodger.

Twenty-Three

At times like this, I truly believed in angels.

Nina had been living with Katrin for several weeks when she thought to mention that she was autistic. 'I don't care,' responded Katrin and by that, Nina knew she meant 'This does not alter my opinion of you, I will treat you just the same.'

Nina enjoyed the blunt style of communication of the Germans she met. She did not believe that it was the language itself that made the Germans more straightforward to communicate with but the culture. In Germany, she found it easier to understand and to be understood. In Britain, she often picked up an underlying passive aggressive tone — a way of belittling, trivialising or minimising what she was trying to say. *Oh, but we've all got a bit of autism in us, haven't we? Everyone feels like that sometimes.* She detected an 'undercurrent of snideness' from some neurotypical people that was impossible to tackle because it was denied. In Germany, however, she did not feel patronised or talked down to, and this made her feel much more secure.

I wrote an article for the *Daily Telegraph* headlined 'I'm so happy that my Nina is miles away'.

This was true but also false. I was delighted that Nina had wanted to go and proud that she was managing once there, but the hypervigilance did not go away. It had become part of me.

One day, we were out for a meal and Cello looked at his phone then gave a sharp intake of breath 'Aw, no...' and I stopped moving, stopped even breathing. Everything around me stilled. What was it? What had happened? Where did I need to go?! What did I need to do?!

I was in immediate crisis mode.

Cello continued studying his phone until I could stand it no longer 'Well?' I said, 'What is it?!' and he shook his head:

'Celtic were a goal up but lost a penalty before half time,' and I slumped, then started to breathe again, trying to quiet my thundering heart.

Twenty-odd years after marrying an Italian, I was still trying to master the Italian language. In a lesson, we were talking about family relationships and the act of caring, for the young, for the old, for those who need us. The teacher, Giulia, said, 'We call it *Lavoro di cura*'. I misheard and thought she said '*Lavoro di cuoro*'. Work of the heart.

'Yes!' I said, 'that's it! – That is exactly what it is: *lavoro di cuoro.*'

I felt it. The Work of the Heart. I knew it. I recognised it. I had done it: mothering the truest heart-work of all.

Nina graduated from Edinburgh University in a ceremony at the McEwan Hall in 2017. I went along with Cello and his brother Rino – the uncle who had drawn endless Teletubbies when Nina was two, and who had taken her to the butterfly farm despite hating creepy crawlies when she was five and who had given her lifts home from Steiners in her teens – and we took our places high, high up, right at the back. There was a spare place beside us because at the last minute Lara couldn't make it – she was on a bus that was dropping off autistic children from a summer school where she was working, but the bus had got caught in traffic that was heading to the royal garden party at Holyrood Palace, traffic that was circling hopelessly looking for parking spaces. As she silently cursed the Queen's tottering, wind-blown, over-dressed guests, she led the children in rousing choruses of *Old MacDonald had a Farm*, and the wheels on the bus did indeed go round and round, but sadly only haltingly; stop-starting too slowly to get her to the graduation on time.

Twenty-Three

Meanwhile, we sat in the newly refurbished Italian Renaissance-style McEwan Hall, below its sumptuous dome with the painting of The Temple of Fame, depicting figures from the arts and sciences.

The floor of the hall was a sea of black graduation gowns with different coloured hoods, but I soon spotted Nina right at the front near the end of the row: only second up to collect her scroll. A scroll that had seemed unattainable when she was fourteen when her mental health had been pushed to the edge of collapse and she had been bullied out of the local high school.

At the end of the graduation ceremony, the dignitary officiating made a speech praising the hard work of the graduates, but then added that none of their success would have been possible without those of us in the audience who had supported them on the way. He suggested they turn and give us a wave.

From our bench high at the back, I watched Nina at the front jump up and turn, bouncing on her toes as she lifted both arms, her graduation gown flowing as she gave a great full-length wave, waving and waving at us, not drowning now but definitely waving, a picture of happiness across this wide-open space.

The cheers from students and parents alike echoed under the dome. Around the base of the dome was written, in gold leaf: Wisdom is the principal thing, therefore get wisdom, and with all thy getting get understanding. Exalt her and she shall bring thee to honour.

And I know that any wisdom I have gathered along the way, and any understanding I have garnered about how to survive this life, and make meaning from it, has been achieved through the act of raising my children.

Hold Fast

My children had been, and remain, my greatest teachers.

The whole hall was cheering and waving. Every family only had eyes for their own graduating child, perhaps remembering their own stories, reflecting on the days, or the weeks, when they too could hardly believe they would ever reach this moment here today, this moment of celebration, this moment of pure joy.

Acknowledgments

With thanks to:
My agent, Joanna Swainson of Hardman & Swainson.
Sara Hunt and all at Saraband.
Cello, Nina and Lara, and everyone who helped us throughout this story – especially Rino for all the Teletubbies you drew. Thank you.

CATHERINE SIMPSON is a novelist and memoir writer based in Edinburgh. Her memoir *One Body* was published by Saraband in 2022 and was selected for World Book Night in 2023 and shortlisted in Scotland's National Book Awards. This followed her 2019 memoir, *When I Had a Little Sister*, which was published to great critical acclaim: 'Superb' *(Sunday Times)*; 'Riveting' *(Observer)*. Her debut novel, *Truestory*, was published in 2015 and won her a Scottish Book Trust New Writers Award. Her work has been broadcast on BBC Radio 4 and BBC Radio Scotland.